Work in Brexit Britain

Reshaping the nation's labour market

Edited by Stephen Clarke

Contents

Introduction

Almost a year after voting to leave the European Union the negotiations for the UK's departure have finally begun. Those negotiations and the exact nature of the agreements they lead to will dominate British politics and policy making for the years ahead. Making a success of Brexit Britain however is about far more than the text in new international treaties.

This is partly because Brexit itself brings with it big shifts in many parts of our national life, and indeed the lives of British firms, families and individuals that require responses. But it is also because with or without Brexit there are wider challenges and opportunities facing us.

Brexit and wider economic issues, some of which drove the decision to leave the EU, look set to come together with some force in our labour market in the coming years. Indeed, as this book sets out, the combination of these shifts mean that parts of the UK economy are at a tipping point.

The UK economy is about to face a dual shock of big increases in the relative cost of low paid labour and a potential reduction in the supply of it. A rising National Living Wage (NLW), auto enrolment and other increases in business costs will overlap at the bottom of our labour market with falling migration. Firms that have previously relied on low-wage labour will see challenges posed to their current choice of business model. For the sectors and firms involved that means wrestling with serious questions about what they produce and how they produce it. For the government it means ensuring that delivering Brexit means more than just signing the right bit of paper at the end of long-winded negotiations.

This book discusses these forces and how businesses and policy makers might rise to the challenges they pose. The first chapter explains why our labour market may have reached a tipping point, with an increase in the relative cost of low-wage labour and a fall in supply as migration levels reduce. Chapter 2 focuses on that second shift, noting that migration levels are falling long before we formally exit the EU. Chapter 3 discusses how businesses may react to these forces, mapping the varying scope for investment in skills and automation in different sectors. Chapter 4 turns to what the government can do to offset any fall in labour supply by supporting those furthest from the labour market. Chapter 5 outlines how we can tackle high levels of precarious jobs and get our labour market ready for the new world of work, while Chapter 6 focuses on how we can begin to address the UK's endemic challenge of progression out of low pay.

None of these challenges are easy to address and the temptation will be to ignore them while the country navigates its departure from the EU. However this would be a grave mistake. After all, it is through the labour market that many people will in practice experience both the fact of that departure and the nature of it. For most people the abstractions of treaties are nothing compared to the work they do and the firm they do it in. That is why addressing the challenges and seizing the opportunities set out in this book in tandem with the exit negotiations is central to laying the foundations for a successful post-Brexit labour market.

David Willetts, Executive Chair of the Resolution Foundation

CHAPTER ONE

End of an era?

The supply of low-wage labour is set to fall
and its price is set to rise

Torsten Bell & Stephen Clarke

Labour markets change. They can do so slowly, in the face of deep-rooted structural trends; or quickly, following big policy moves or shifts in the economic cycle. Even before last year's Brexit vote the UK labour market was displaying signs of change on all three of these fronts: long-term wage and employment relationships looked to be changing; a tightening labour market appeared to challenge the assumed permanency of some trends towards insecurity; and a huge policy shift was underway in the form of a significantly raised wage floor with the introduction of the National Living Wage (NLW). Add in the Brexit process, and in particular the prospect of a significant reduction in the availability of migrant labour, and the UK labour market starts to look as though it's approaching a potential tipping point.

Importantly, these developments appear to be concentrated towards the bottom end of the labour market. The pay squeeze that started after the financial crisis continues to be an issue across large parts of the earnings distribution, with the current decade on course to be the worst for average pay growth in over 200 years.[1] However, as we move down the earnings distribution we find that wages – and broader labour costs – are bucking the trend. It is also in that part of the labour market that migrant labour is concentrated and therefore where major post-Brexit migration policy shifts might have most impact.

For those firms reliant on relatively low paid labour, the impact of these two shifts will be significant: an era of seemingly limitless and relatively inexpensive low paid labour may be coming to an end. Understanding just what this potential tipping point might mean for firms' business models and our nation's labour market – rather than worries about the arrival of robots bringing an end to the world of work – should form the main focus of policy makers' attention as we prepare for post-Brexit Britain.

This book aims to chart the coming change. Not because the exact impact can be predicted, but because very different outcomes are possible on the basis of different decisions by government and firms that engage with, and shape, our labour market.

Much has changed in the UK labour market since 2008

Digging into the changes that are underway in our labour market can save us from one of the most common errors in public policy making: assuming that tomorrow's battles look just like those of today. The importance of learning this lesson was brought out clearly by the post-financial crisis experience, which departed significantly from expectations.

In late-2008 it became clear that the UK was facing a significant recession, with output contracting by over 2 per cent in the final quarter of that year alone. All planning in Whitehall focused on what history told us would be the single biggest challenge from a recession on this scale – unemployment shooting up and topping three million, with lasting damage to the individuals concerned and the productive capacity of the UK economy.

Although unemployment did increase it never approached the highs recorded in the late 1970s, and as Figure 1 shows, employment returned to its pre-crisis peak much faster than in previous recessions. Clearly this was a welcome development, not least as rising employment benefitted those on lower incomes the most. Importantly, post-crisis employment growth has been about more than just unwinding cyclical unemployment. Rather, we have seen an increase in the number of people *participating* in the labour market, lifting the employment rate well above its pre-crisis levels.

The widespread availability of labour has been reinforced by an even faster growth in the number of hours worked per person. Both have been buttressed by a substantial rise in the labour supply coming from abroad during this period; migrants have accounted for two-thirds of the growth in employment over the past five years.

Figure 1: **A tale of three recessions: 1979, 1990 & 2008**

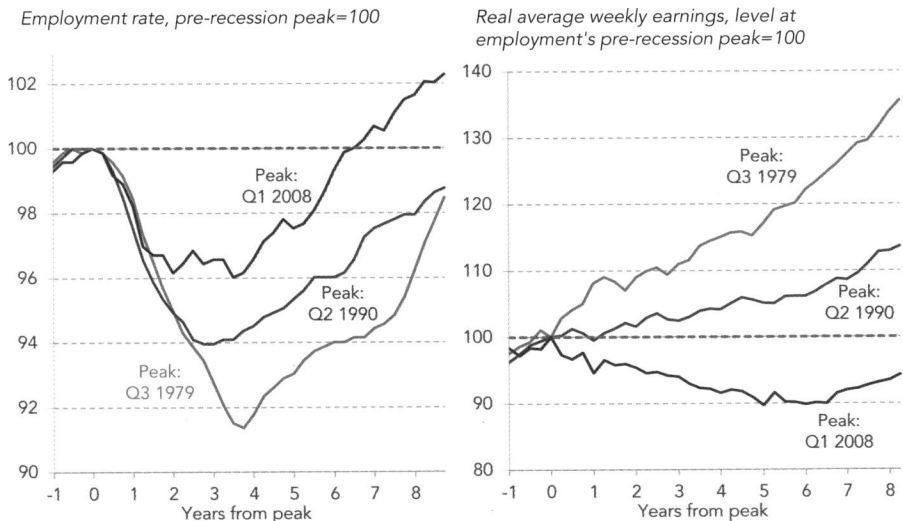

Employment rate, pre-recession peak=100

Real average weekly earnings, level at employment's pre-recession peak=100

Source: RF analysis of Bank of England, *Three Centuries of Data*

Alongside the jobs 'boom' however, Britain has faced a post-crisis productivity and pay 'bust'. As the right-hand panel of Figure 1 makes clear, employees have endured an entirely unexpected and unprecedented period of not just slowing but falling wages. Only in Greece has the post-crisis squeeze on earnings been as dramatic.[2] Earnings remain 6 per cent lower than they were in early 2008 and productivity has only grown by 1.5 per cent in a decade, well below the 2.3 per cent annual growth experienced before the crisis. This was something unseen in previous recessions and something policy makers had made no preparations for.

End of an era?

Policy has also been slow to catch up with the large post-crisis rise in atypical or insecure work towards the bottom of the labour market. Since 2008 the number of people on zero hours contracts (ZHCs) has risen significantly to 900,000, agency workers have increased by 46 per cent, while some (but far from all) of the spectacular growth in self-employment has certainly been at the insecure end.

Taken together then, much has changed since the financial crisis. Unforeseen though it was in 2008, Britain has now got used to the idea that labour is available, that it is cheap and that – at the bottom of the labour market – it is prepared to work without the normal security of standard full-time employment.

More change is coming, thanks to a relative price shock at the bottom end of the labour market

Yet, just as policy makers were caught out by developments after 2008, so a failure to update our understanding of the labour market in light of more recent developments risks meaning we misdiagnose the challenges of the coming years. In particular, shifts at the bottom end of the workforce could underpin profound changes in the functioning of our labour market. Below we'll consider the effect of a potential labour supply shock associated with Brexit. But first we discuss the effects of a relative price shock that is already becoming apparent.

While there is no sign of an end to the UK's overall pay squeeze,[3] there are good grounds for believing that firms who employ low paid workers will face fairly fast rises in their labour costs over the coming years.

First and foremost, the roll-out of the NLW imposes a direct cost on those hiring workers at or near the wage floor. The NLW is set to rise much more quickly than typical earnings over its first few years, such that its value reaches 60 per cent of median 25 and over earnings in 2020 (after which it will rise in line with typical earnings growth). An expected real increase of 10 per cent between now and 2020 (taking it to £8.75) is significantly more rapid than either the 3.5 per cent expected for average earnings over the same period or the norm for the National Minimum Wage over the previous 15 years.

The scale of the impact of the NLW on relative labour costs is apparent in Figure 2. It shows that earnings rose by between

By 2020, we project that 15 per cent of all employees will be on the National Living Wage

4 and 6 per cent for the bottom 30 per cent of the earnings distribution between April 2015 and April 2016 (the point at which the NLW was introduced). By 2020, we project that 15 per cent of all employees will be on the NLW, increasing the wage bill for those firms affected by £4.5 billion. Crucially, this will represent not just an absolute cost increase for firms but a relative one too, with employees at the bottom end of the labour market costing more relative to both higher paid workers and to capital.

Figure 2: **Pay growth has been strong for low earners: 2015-2016**

Increase in real gross weekly pay (CPIH adjusted)

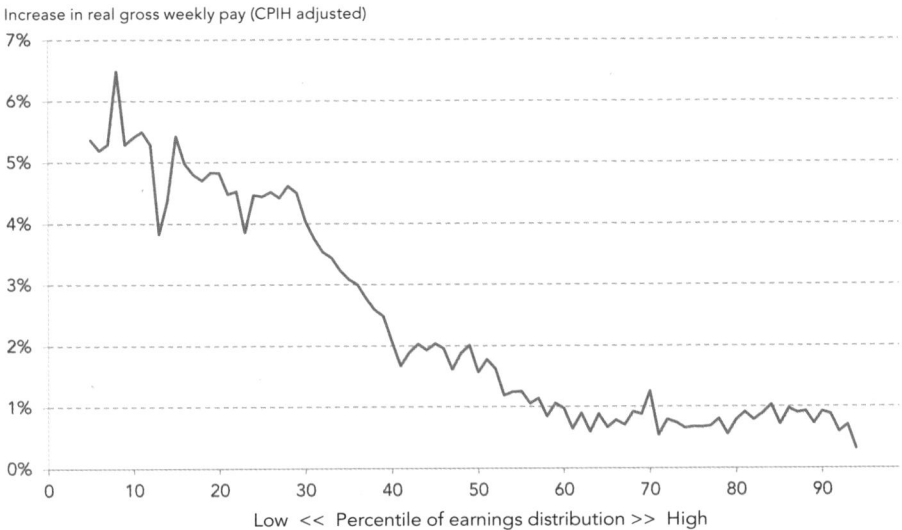

Low << Percentile of earnings distribution >> High

Source: RF analysis of ONS, *ASHE*

We would of course expect those sectors that rely most on cheap labour to be most affected by the lifting of the wage floor. In some industries, such as hospitality and retail, half of all employees look set to be affected by 2020. As such, wage bills in these sectors could rise by 3 per cent or more, as Table 1 shows. The early evidence we have suggests that labour costs are indeed rising most rapidly in those sectors listed at the top of Table 1. Real labour costs have risen by an average of 2.6 per cent in wholesale, retail, hotels and restaurants since the introduction of the NLW. They have also risen by 4 per cent in the construction industry, though given the large amount of self-employment in this sector other factors have likely played a part. By contrast they have risen by just 0.7 per cent for the private sector overall, and have fallen in finance and business services.[4]

Alongside the direct wage costs associated with the NLW, firms are also facing higher labour costs from other aspects of government policy – including the ramping up of auto-enrolment pension saving and the apprenticeship levy.[5] These represent more generalised costs than the NLW, but the former is likely to weigh heavier at the bottom of the labour market.

Since 2012, firms have been required to enrol all staff onto company pension schemes and to contribute to them. Larger firms were first to face the obligation, but all firms will by April 2018. The amount firms must contribute will also increase over time, from 1 per cent of an employee's earnings to 3 per cent. While firms do not have to contribute for those earning less than £5,876 per annum and those earning less than £10,000 or under 22 do not have to be enrolled (but can request to be), the evidence to date is that lower paid staff have benefited disproportionately from the move – presumably because higher earners were much more likely to already have access to an occupational pension scheme. For example, the number of people earning less than £300 a week and on a defined contribution pension scheme rose by 250 per cent between 2012 and 2016, compared with an increase of 86 per cent for those earning £500 or more.

The Department for Work and Pensions estimates that by 2019-20 employers will have to contribute an extra £6 billion annually in pension contributions as a result of the auto-enrolment policy. The scale of the impact is therefore likely to be equivalent to that of the NLW.

Coming together, these various – very welcome – policies will significantly raise the relative price of low-wage labour, compared to both higher-paid workers and the cost of capital. The impact of this shock will be felt differently across sectors, but will bring with it a strong incentive to think hard about how that labour is used.

The bottom end of the labour market may also be further affected by a labour supply shock associated with Brexit

The UK's recent jobs 'boom' owes something to both a rebound from the unemployment sparked by the financial crisis and increases in participation among older workers and other groups such as single parents. But it is also a product of sizeable increases in net migration over the past decade. The arrival of large numbers of foreign workers has provided a major boost to the UK's GDP and eased a wide range of labour shortages, both sectorally and geographically. Yet, as with costs at the bottom end of the labour market, things look to be changing.

Currently, residents of European Union (EU) and European Economic Area (EEA) countries can freely move to the UK. Since this right was enshrined in 1992, and particularly since the A8[6] countries joined the EU in 2004, many Europeans have come to the UK for work. Migrants from the EU and EEA account for only 7 per cent of all employment, yet workers from the continent have become an increasingly important part of the labour market, particularly since 2004. Since this point the number of people from the EU in work in the UK has increased by 1.6 million and migrants from the A8 countries have accounted for over 60 per cent of this increase. More recently, EU migrants have accounted for a third of the increase in employment since 2010.

In some sectors migrants are an even larger part of the labour force, forming a large proportion of employees in hospitality, agriculture and a large share of domestic workers. EU migrants form 15 per cent of employment in the food manufacturing industry, 13 per cent of hotel employees and 9 per cent of all restaurant and bar staff. The figures in Table 1 exclude the self-employed and so probably underrepresent the

Table 1: **Increasing costs for firms: 2016 & 2020**

Sector	Increase in wage bill in 2020 as a result of the NLW	EU migrants as a share of employees (2016)
Food and beverage service activities	3.6%	8.9%
Services to buildings and landscape	3.0%	8.5%
Accommodation	2.8%	12.5%
Residential care activities	2.8%	3.9%
Manufacture of wearing apparel	2.6%	6.6%
Security and investigation activities	2.3%	3.0%
Employment activities	2.0%	5.6%
Retail trade, except vehicles	2.0%	3.8%
Crop, animal production, hunting	1.9%	7.0%
Other personal service activities	1.9%	4.1%
Gambling and betting activities	1.8%	4.5%
Manufacture of textiles	1.8%	5.1%
Manufacture of food products	1.4%	15.2%
Domestic personnel	1.3%	16.9%
Manufacture of furniture	1.3%	5.9%
Social work without accommodation	1.3%	3.6%
Wholesale and retail trade	1.2%	3.0%
Sports, amusement, recreation	0.9%	3.9%
Manufacture of wood and wood products	0.8%	4.8%
Rental and leasing activities	0.8%	4.3%

Source: RF analysis of ONS, *ASHE* and *LFS*

migrant workforce in some sectors – such as construction – where self-employment is common. Geographic concentration also means that in some parts of the country they form an even greater part of the workforce than this.

As well as the variation across the economy, what stands out is the extent to which many of the sectors most reliant on migrant labour are also significantly affected by the NLW. The sectors in Table 1 will be those most affected by changes in the labour market, they all have an above-average exposure to increases in the NLW and the majority of them also have an above-average proportion of EU migrant employees. Figure 3 reinforces the point that many lower paying sectors will feel the dual impact of a rising NLW and falling migration. The share of EU migrants earning between £220 and £340 (£60 a week either side of full-time earnings on NLW) is 50 per cent greater

Figure 3: **EU migrants tend to cluster towards the lower part of the earnings distribution: 2014-2016**

Share of earners by weekly earnings

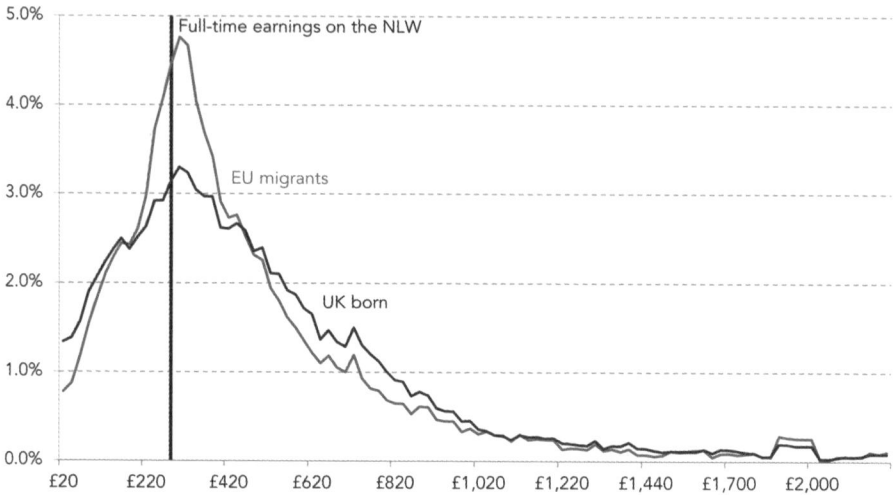

Notes: Weekly earnings capped at those earning £3,000 or above.

Source: RF analysis of ONS, *LFS*

than that for natives. Around a third of EU migrants sit in this part of the distribution compared to a fifth of natives.

Migrants have therefore played an important role in the country's recent employment boom, increasing the availability of relatively skilled, flexible labour. In some sectors they carry out tasks that native workers cannot or do not wish to do. They have also increased the geographical mobility of labour in the UK, further boosting effective labour supply beyond the levels implied by the raw number of workers. This is both because they are more mobile once they are based in the UK but also because migrants tend to go to places that have tight labour markets in the first place.[7]

The impact of migration on wages is hotly debated. Our own evidence, in common with wider work, finds no effect on wages overall but a small effect on lower paid and lower skilled workers.[8] In any given year that effect is negligible and is clearly dominated by wider shifts in productivity or employment, but over a prolonged period it is not immaterial.

Looking to the future the combination of the decision to leave the European Union (EU), the fact that both Labour and the Conservatives have promised to end freedom of movement, and a tightening labour market in many European countries means that the years ahead are likely to bring big changes to the role of migration in the UK labour market.

While the full impact of the Brexit vote on immigration will not be felt for many years, there are some early signs that numbers are already easing off. Figures for the end of 2016 show that net migration dropped below 250,000 for the first time in three years, National Insurance registrations for EU workers are flat, and there has been a plateauing in those born in the EU working in the UK.[9] While the data is not yet suggesting a dramatic drop in EU workers, some industries have suggested that they may soon face significant shortages.[10]

Further reductions are likely even ahead of any major migration policy changes if the wider European economy continues to perform strongly, the pound remains relatively weak and uncertainty exists about EU migrants' ability to stay in the UK long term.

In terms of the first of these factors – one that is often less discussed in the UK – the evidence is that over the past year labour markets in Europe have begun to tighten significantly. This is true both in countries such as Germany and other European nations that tend to attract economic migrants, but also in countries used to seeing significant emigration. Across the whole of the EU (excluding the UK) the unemployment rate has fallen from just below 10 per cent to just below 8 per cent, with some countries, particularly Poland and Bulgaria, experiencing a more significant decline (Figure 4).

Migrants have therefore played an important part in the country's recent employment boom

Given the continued strength of many European economies, further tightening in the future is likely, however regardless of conditions in Europe, eventually Brexit will provide the government with the policy flexibility to control immigration from the EU, further tightening the labour supply. The Conservatives have promised a significant reduction in migration as a key objective of the new government. The Labour party have not committed to a specific migration target or such a significant decline in migration, but nevertheless support the end of free movement.

The fact that lower paying sectors are currently most reliant on migrants means that this tightening of labour supply will overlap with the parts of the economy already seeing increased labour costs in the next few years. Indeed, the migrant earnings picture set out in Figure 3 would be even more skewed towards low earners if we restricted our analysis to temporary, or short-term migrants – those most likely to be affected by any future changes to the country's immigration system.

At the bottom end of the labour market, the supply shock associated with reduced migration will therefore compound the pressures already facing firms as a result of rising labour costs. The implication is that firms in the most affected sectors will need to make more significant changes to what they do or how they do it – be that replacing migrant workers with natives, substituting capital for labour or ceasing to produce certain things – than would be warranted by the presence of either a price or a supply shock in isolation.

Figure 4: **A tightening labour market in Europe will further reduce migration**

Unemployment rates for the EU and selected EU countries

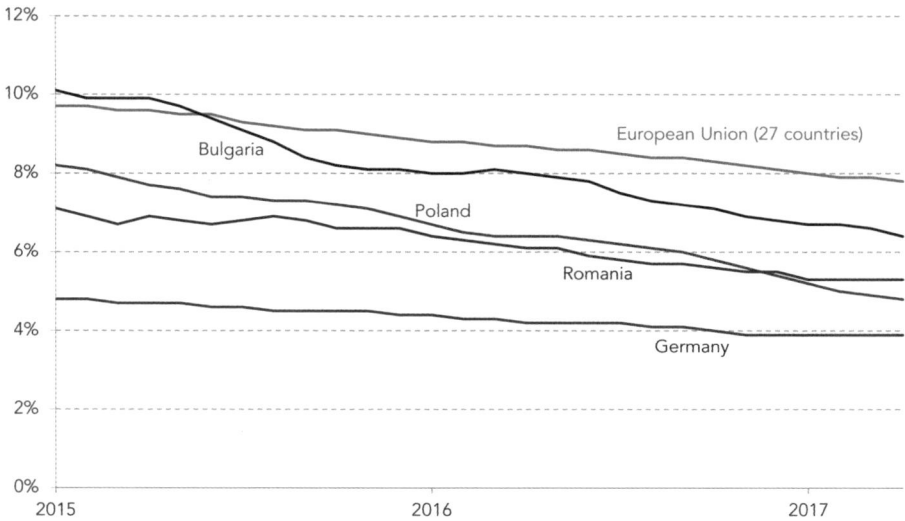

Source: RF analysis of Eurostat, *Unemployment*

A tighter labour market may already be affecting the types of jobs people are doing, if not their pay

The pressures associated with this dual shock can be expected to build over the coming years. Yet we may already be starting to see some effects manifest themselves in the form of a modest reversal in the trend towards atypical (or insecure) work.

Growth in insecure work over the course of the 21st century is often described as a product of either advancing technology or people's wish for more flexibility. The latter is viewed as empowering, while the former is usually considered demoralising. But both explanations are used to underpin an expectation that insecure work will simply grow year on year. Yet we have begun to see the number of people employed in atypical forms of work flattening out or even falling over the last 12 months.

The number of people on ZHCs reached 900,000 in early 2016, but has not risen since, while the number of agency workers has *fallen* to 800,000, having hit a high of 850,000 last year. And the share of all workers accounted for by self-employment has also started to fall since the turn of the year – reversing a previously consistently increasing trend. In contrast, those working full time for an employer have accounted for 97 per cent of the growth in employment in the past year.

Work in Brexit Britain

While it is obviously early days, these numbers could be consistent with a tightening of the labour market. And to the extent that atypical working is often associated with lower paying roles, we might speculate that today's tightening is being felt most acutely at the bottom end of the labour market. Indeed, in interviews with businesses we've heard that some firms have responded to the introduction of the NLW by lowering their use of ZHCs, arguing that higher labour costs necessitate the establishment of more permanent – and higher quality – relationships with their workers.[11]

The presence of significant numbers of atypical jobs in the post-crisis labour market could help to explain why we haven't yet seen impressive reductions in unemployment drive up wages in any significant way. A lot of work has been done to try and explain this ongoing riddle,[12] with the most popular explanations highlighting subdued productivity growth and a range of reasons for believing there could be more slack in the labour market than the headline employment figures suggest.[13] However, it may well be that the raised level of atypical work in our economy post-crisis means that the labour market tightening is feeding through in the first instance to changes in the types of jobs people do, rather than their pay. That is, as workers gain more power and employers find it harder to fill vacancies, the first thing that is demanded and conceded is greater security rather than higher pay.

It is important to recognise that the level of insecure work remains too high in Britain today and that there are a range of areas where labour market regulation should be changed to tackle it, as Chapter 4 sets out. But, while recognising that fact, we need to be careful in assuming that a key feature of our labour market is ever-rising insecurity. Firms assuming they will simply be able to continue employing more people on such terms may well find themselves disappointed in the years ahead. This will necesitate adjustments not just in the contracts firms offer but in entire business models in some cases.

> The next five years will bring with them a raft of changes that will impact the UK's labour market

The times they are a-changin'

Discussions of the UK labour market have focused in recent years on the abundant supply of cheap labour, a growing proportion of which has been prepared to work with less security than many workers take for granted. These trends have been particularly pronounced at the bottom of the labour market. But just because that story has held in recent years, firms and policy makers shouldn't simply assume such trends will continue.

The next five years will bring with them a raft of changes that will impact the UK's labour market. We have highlighted some of the main ones that, combined, may well mean that we are at a tipping point when it comes to the availability and cost of low paid labour.[14] This represents a big change for our economy, and one we would do well to prepare for. The changes may bring welcome pay rises for millions of people and the opportunity to make some of our firms and sectors more productive and higher paying. But they also carry big risks of employment shifts, labour shortages and lost output if we get things wrong.

First and foremost, it is firms themselves that will respond to the increased cost of low paid labour and its reduced availability – changing what they produce and how they produce it. Quite how these employers will react is not yet clear. Focusing solely on the cost increases associated with the initial introduction of the NLW, our research has shown that around a third of firms raised prices, with around one in seven firms investing more in training and around one in eight investing more in technology.[15] This may be an indication of what firms will do when faced with wider price and supply pressures in the coming years, although over time a wider range of adjustment strategies should be available.

But government has a clear role too. Not only because it lies behind the scale and pace of several of the changes affecting firms, but also because the coming challenges raise broader questions for the country at large. Despite the uncertainty created by a hung parliament, the government owes business more clarity about the world in which they will be operating, and should be providing an impetus to the sectors most affected to get on with necessary adjustments.

Perhaps the most important issue that needs to be clarified soon is what the country's immigration system will be after we leave the EU (Chapter 2). Clarity will allow businesses to take long-term decisions around skills and investment (Chapter 3). Adjusting to a changing labour market also means grappling with new challenges. In a tight labour market increasing labour supply involves supporting those furthest from the labour market (Chapter 4), regulations and rights need to adjust to the new world of work (Chapter 5) and the UK's entrenched reliance on low pay remains a problem (Chapter 6). This section has outlined the changes that the UK economy is facing, but the rest of the book addresses the harder question of how it can rise to the challenges ahead.

1   M Whittaker et al., *Are we nearly there yet? Spring Budget 2017 and the 15 year squeeze on family and public finances*, Resolution Foundation, March 2017

2   S Clarke & C D'Arcy, *Low Pay Britain 2016*, Resolution Foundation, October 2016

3   M Whittaker et al., *Are we nearly there yet? Spring Budget 2017 and the 15 year squeeze on family and public finances*, Resolution Foundation, March 2017

4   ONS, *Index of Labour Costs per Hour (ILCH): Oct to Dec 2016*, June 2017

5   The Office for Budget Responsibility expects that the levy will bring in around £3 billion per annum. However, it will only affect firms with a pay bill of £3 million or above and will not have a differential effect on the cost of lower paid workers.

6   Czech Republic, Estonia, Hungary, Latvia, Lithuania, Poland, Slovak Republic and Slovenia.

7   RF analysis of ONS, *LFS*

8   S Clarke, *A Brave New World: how reduced migration could affect earnings, employment and the labour market*, Resolution Foundation, August 2016

9   S Clarke, *First signs of falling migration after the Brexit vote*, March 2017

10   The Observer, "Record numbers of EU nurses quit NHS", 18 March 2017; The Guardian, "Farmers deliver stark warning over access to EU seasonal workers", 21 February 2017.

11   C D'Arcy & G Davies, *Weighing up the wage floor: Employer responses to the National Living Wage*, Resolution Foundation, February 2016

12   A Haldane, *'Twin Peaks', speech for Kenilworth Chamber of Trade Business Breakfast*, 17 October 2014

13   M Saunders, *'New Year, New Labour market? What does 2017 have to offer'*, Keynote speech by MPC member Michael Saunders at the Resolution Foundation, January 2017

14   Other likely changes include shifts in the tax regime for the self-employed, a possible reform of the employee-worker distinction and the roll out of Universal Credit.

15   C D'Arcy & M Whittaker, *The first 100 days: early evidence on the impact of the National Living Wage*, July 2016

CHAPTER TWO

Filling in the gaps

Preparing for the end of free movement

Stephen Clarke

The state we're in

Migrants or those born outside the UK account for 18 per cent of people in work and have accounted for two-thirds of the growth in employment over the past five years

Nearly half of firms we polled expect free movement to continue or that all immigrants with a job offer will be able to move to the UK

Net migration has fallen to below 250,000 for the first time in three years

What should we do?

The government needs to provide a clear vision for the country's future immigration system well before the point at which the UK leaves the EU

The MAC needs greater resources and a broader role in deciding what skills immigration needs to provide

A streamlined system for skilled EU/EEA migrants, temporary worker schemes, and more investment in enforcement are all likely to be needed

I t is the combined effect of the shifts discussed in the previous chapter that could add up to a turning point in the availability and cost of labour at the bottom of Britain's labour market. But the certainty with which we can predict the elements of these shifts varies significantly. The scale and pace of increases to the National Living Wage are fairly clear right through until 2022 – even if their impact is not. In contrast there is huge uncertainty about the other big shift coming to the UK labour market – the pace and nature of a reduction in migration. Significant policy uncertainty about the UK's post-Brexit migration regime combines with the complexity of how individuals and firms change their behaviour to make a wide range of outcomes possible.

This chapter focuses on this uncertainty, the questions that the decision to leave the EU raises about the UK's approach to immigration, the implications for the labour market, and the fact that many firms appear wholly unprepared for the way in which immigration is likely to decline in future. This is intentionally a partial labour market focus, leaving aside other important debates about the public finances, public service use and wider social impacts.

Upon leaving the EU the government will be able to impose restrictions on immigration from the continent. The Conservatives have promised to use this new-found freedom to significantly reduce net migration, perhaps by as much as two-thirds from its current level. By contrast Labour have not committed to reducing migration by any specific amount, but have promised to 'manage' migration and end freedom of movement. Both parties have provided very few specific details about how the immigration system will function after we leave the EU.

Meanwhile there are already signs that migration is falling and new research for this publication highlights the fact that firms are woefully under-prepared for a significant change. Now is therefore the time for the government to set out the future immigration system that businesses should be preparing to operate within. That means going beyond generalities about lower overall numbers, or more managed migration, to providing clarity on the time-frame for change, what types of migrants will no longer be permitted to move to the UK and what, if any, transitional arrangements will help businesses and the economy adjust. This chapter sets out some broad principles that should be front of mind as the government seeks to change the country's immigration system. For the purposes of this chapter we take that change as a given, assuming the new government is able to deliver on their policy intentions.

> Migration has ebbed and flowed over the course of the last two decades

Migrants form a significant part of the UK labour market

These are not small issues for our labour market. Migrants[1] play a significant part in the UK's economy and labour market – in terms of scale, growth in labour supply and flexibility.

Migration has ebbed and flowed over the course of the last two decades. Change has been driven by a number of factors including; the state of the UK's economy, the country's immigration regime and the situation in other countries. Figure 1 shows that net migration (on the left-hand axis) rose steadily from the mid-1990s, spurred by the relative performance of the British economy and value of the pound. There was a sharp increase after 2004 when the A8 countries joined the EU and the number of A8 workers in the labour force rose sharply. Numbers dipped from the financial crisis until 2014, when net migration rose to new highs until the EU referendum, following which it has fallen. As a result of rising net migration the number of migrants in the labour force (right-hand axis) has also risen.

The result is that today 18 per cent of all people in work were born abroad. Migrants play an even more significant role in the growth of labour supply than in the stock; migrants account for two-thirds of the increase in employment over the past five years.

Figure 1: **Migration and the numbers of migrants in the UK labour force**

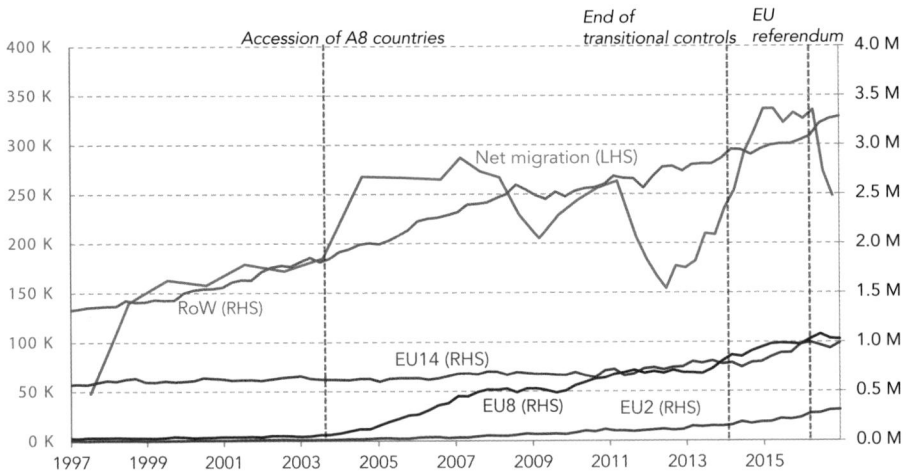

Source: RF analysis of ONS, *LFS* and *International Passenger Survey (IPS)*

For the size of the UK economy in aggregate these are very significant numbers. But migration has not only increased the overall size of the UK labour force, it has also increased its flexibility. For example it has increased the geographic mobility of our labour force: migrants are much more likely, as much as twice as likely in the case of EU migrants, to move regions than natives. Furthermore migrants tend to go to parts of the UK labour market that are tightest in the first place; migrants form between a third and a half of all residents in many London boroughs. In addition, migrants respond quickly to changes in demand; migrant populations have increased fastest in many parts of the country that heavily rely on temporary, flexible labour. [2]

Readily available migrant labour, with low costs of hiring in the case of workers from within the EU, has also played a significant role in reducing labour and skill shortages. Its existence will also have affected decisions taken by firms in terms of what to produce and what investments in capital and training are needed.

So taken together migration has meant a bigger, faster growing and more flexible labour supply in recent years. It has also meant British firms becoming used to the availability of plentiful, flexible labour. Given this, any significant change in migration is likely to have a big and complex impact on our labour market.

Work in Brexit Britain

From current high levels it is likely migration numbers will fall in future

We believe Britain is set for just such a change. Although the scale of that change is not yet clear it is likely that the country will see a shift in migration numbers in both the relatively near future and more structurally following post-Brexit changes in the migration regime.

The Conservative government's explicit recent reaffirmation of their commitment to reduce net migration to the tens of thousands (alongside promises in their manifesto to increase the earnings thresholds for people wishing to sponsor migrants for family visas and increases in the costs of employing non-EU/EEA workers), combined with policy freedom to restrict EU and EEA migration (the Brexit White Paper stated that in the future the country will control the numbers of people coming to the UK from the EU[3]) means that it is reasonable to assume migration could fall significantly.

Net migration has already fallen from a high of 335,000 to 248,000

The Labour party have not committed to such a significant reduction but have promised to end freedom of movement, with new controls imposed on EU migration. Although many changes will not happen until we depart the EU, the fall in the value of Sterling – down 12 per cent in trade-weighted terms since the vote to leave the EU – and the fact that many immigrants may perceive the UK as less welcoming or may feel unsure about their right to remain in the country, could mean a decline comes earlier.[4]

Indeed as shown in Figure 1 net migration has already fallen from a high of 335,000 to 248,000. Recent data suggests that the number of EU14 and EU8 migrants in the labour force may have plateaued but the referendum has had no discernible effect on the numbers of Bulgarian and Romanian workers. The absolute size of changes to date is not yet substantial, so it is not surprising that in a new mid-April 2017 survey for this publication of around 500 firms that employ EU/EEA migrants, two-thirds reported that they had seen no change in the number of migrants they employ. However such evidence does not exclude the possibility that specific sectors have experienced shortages. The agricultural sector (see Box 3), food manufacturing and the health service have all voiced concerns that they are having trouble finding staff.[5]

Changes in migration will affect some sectors much more than others

If net migration falls it is likely that those sectors that are particularly reliant on migrant labour will feel the pinch first. Table 1 shows that nearly four in ten employers in the food manufacturing sector and a similar proportion of domestic workers were born abroad. One in three employees in hotels, bars and restaurants are migrants with a significant proportion of these coming from the EU. Despite not being the focus of this publication it is worth noting that some higher paid sectors also have sizeable migrant

Table 1: **Some industries are very reliant on migrant labour: 2014-2016**

Industry	Share of total employment (%)				
	EU14	EU8	EU2	RoW	All migrants
Manufacture of food products	4.1%	9.2%	1.8%	26.0%	41.1%
Domestic personnel	6.0%	4.5%	6.3%	22.5%	39.3%
Undifferentiated goods	4.2%	1.7%	4.2%	25.5%	35.6%
Manufacture of wearing apparel	3.3%	2.5%	0.8%	25.0%	31.6%
Accommodation	4.7%	4.7%	3.1%	18.1%	30.5%
Food and beverage service activities	5.1%	2.2%	1.6%	21.2%	30.1%
Extraterritorial organisations	6.1%	0.4%	0.0%	23.1%	29.6%
Security & investigation activities	1.7%	0.6%	0.7%	24.2%	27.2%
Services to buildings and landscape	3.5%	2.3%	2.8%	16.9%	25.5%
Computer programming and consultancy	5.2%	0.5%	0.6%	19.1%	25.4%
Warehousing & support for transport	2.1%	3.5%	1.7%	17.7%	25.0%
Scientific research and development	6.4%	0.5%	0.7%	17.0%	24.6%
Land transport inc via pipelines	3.0%	1.0%	1.0%	18.9%	23.9%
Residential care activities	2.0%	0.7%	1.3%	17.3%	21.2%
Manufacture of textiles	2.3%	2.4%	0.5%	15.7%	20.8%

Source: RF analysis of ONS, *LFS*

workforces – a quarter of employees in computer programming and scientific research were born outside the UK. Sectors with high staff turnover are likely to feel the impact first, and this tends to be higher in lower paying sectors such as hospitality.[6]

Firms appear unprepared and have unrealistic expectations about the UK's future immigration system

The combination of a likely reduction in migration with heavy reliance by some firms on such labour means that significant adjustments to ways of working are likely to be needed in parts of our economy. Those adjustments will take time and need planning for, but there is very little sign of that taking place (see Box 1).

The fact that firms are not expecting big changes in the short term may be understandable given that changes in net migration are about the flow of migrant labour and take time to have a sizable impact on the stock of workers. More concerning looking further ahead however is the risk that firms may be complacent about the scale of the change coming, with the risk that they are left disappointed and surprised by the immigration system eventually adopted, and with insufficient time to make the transition to a new reality.

---

i Box 1: Are firms ready for a fall in migration?

We polled 500 business decision-makers in firms that employed EU/EEA migrants to find out how the fall in migration had affected them in the past six months and if they expected to be affected in the next year.[7] We found:

- In almost half (42 per cent) of the 500 firms at least one in four staff are migrants. The proportion is over half in 13 per cent of firms.
- Three-quarters of firms (73 per cent) expect that a fall in migration would affect their business.
- In the past six months 65 per cent have seen no change in the number of migrants they employ.
- Only a quarter of firms (26 per cent) expect the number of EU/EEA nationals in their workforce to decline in the next year.
- A similar number (24 per cent) actually expect the number to rise.

Firms are aware of the importance of migrants to their business, but do not expect that a fall in migration will affect staffing levels in their firm. There is danger that as a result few are planning for the future and if migration falls faster than expected businesses could be left short of staff.

Figure 2 shows both what firms would *like* to happen and what they *expect* by way of a post-Brexit immigration system. In terms of preferences the outer circle suggests that firms will be disappointed by the commitment to end freedom of movement and be disappointed with any system that significantly limits immigration. Two-thirds (64 per cent) would like to retain freedom of movement or move to a system where all those with a job can migrate. The first of these has been ruled out by both parties, the second is unlikely to be compatible with the Conservative's target of significant reductions in migration and may not differ much in practice from freedom of movement making it hard to square with the Labour party's 2017 manifesto as well.

The migration system the country chooses however should clearly not just be about what firms would like. More concerning therefore than the fact that firms are unlikely to get the migration system they desire, is the fact that there remains a big difference in what firms expect from the government and what is likely to happen. The inner circle shows that half of firms (47 per cent) expect either free movement to continue or that all those with a job offer will be able to migrate to the UK. This is despite the fact that both parties have ruled out freedom of movement and both indicate that government, rather than business, will play a larger role in the immigration system in the future. Therefore migrant-reliant firms making decisions on the basis of either of those two outcomes are likely to underestimate the scale of change to their business that may be required.

Work in Brexit Britain

Figure 2: **Doomed to be disappointed? What businesses want and expect from a future immigration system**

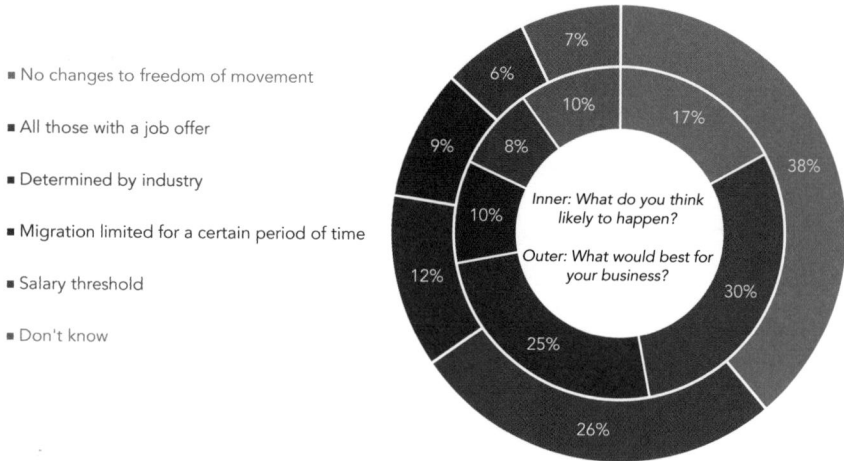

- No changes to freedom of movement
- All those with a job offer
- Determined by industry
- Migration limited for a certain period of time
- Salary threshold
- Don't know

Inner: What do you think likely to happen?

Outer: What would best for your business?

Inner: 7%, 10%, 17%, 38%, 30%, 25%, 12%, 10%, 8%

Outer: 6%, 9%

Base: All business decision-makers employing EU/EEA nationals (n=503)

Source: Prepared by ComRes, fieldwork 12th - 26th April 2017

The government needs to make clear what the key features of the UK's future immigration system are likely to be

To date too much of the debate about migration and the world of work has been polarised between those saying any change is impossible and the government's rhetoric on reductions in numbers. Instead of that we need a focus on how we make whatever regime we choose to adopt (which is not the main topic of this publication) work best for the UK labour market.

British business can function with a wide range of migration regimes, but moving from the status quo to a very different world without unnecessary economic damage requires both clarity on the eventual destination and time to implement changes.

To that end firms will need to adjust their, currently apparently unrealistic, expectations about the UK's future immigration system and government needs to do more to provide clarity about the regime they are aiming for. Designing and running a new immigration system will be a significant bureaucratic challenge (when the current system is already quite complex – see Box 2) taking years not months, but so are the adjustments firms will need to make to operate in a changed labour market, meaning changes not only to how they produce goods and services but to what they produce in the first place. For both reasons, the sooner the broad principles are clear, the better.

---

i Box 2: The current immigration system

For those outside the EU/EAA, there are five tiers to the immigration system for people wishing to come to the UK to work, study, invest or train.

Tier 1 – For 'high-value' migrants, covering entrepreneurs, investors and those who come under the 'exceptional talent' visa. Limited to 1,000 a year, but no limit for investors or entrepreneurs.

Tier 2 – For 'skilled workers' where there is a proven shortage, where a firm can't find a UK or EU/EEA national to do the job, intra-company transfers, and ministers of religion and sportspeople. This is capped at 20,700 a year (although there is no cap for intra-company transfers).

Applicants must have a job offer.

Tier 3 – Designed for low-skilled workers fulling specific labour market shortages. No visas ever allocated under this scheme.

Tier 4 – For students aged 16 and over. Applicants must have a place at a UK educational establishment before they can apply (around 200,000 come through this tier per year).

Tier 5 – Includes six sub-tiers of temporary worker including creative and sporting, charity, religious workers and the youth mobility scheme (around 40,000 visas are granted a year, half of which are for those on the youth mobility scheme).

Deciding on these will be difficult, and the considerations and suggestions we outline below focus on ensuring that disruption in the short-run is minimised and that the eventual system best supports the UK labour market. In this respect we make no judgement on the wider impacts of immigration, although we are aware that the government will need to take into account other concerns, not least public opinion, and the Brexit negotiations. The latter could be particularly important given that whatever system we impose on EU/EEA nationals is likely to heavily affect the regime that UK workers wishing to migrate to the EU will face and to shape elements of any eventual free trade deal.[8]

Providing the skills the UK economy needs

Moving away from a world of a very large and varied pool of potential migrant labour with relatively low hiring costs and bureaucracy, to a much more controlled system will put significantly more pressure on government decision making and intelligence. The Conservative party says that it wants to make the immigration system work for sectors facing skills shortages and the Labour party have also said any future system should reflect economic needs. However, because the existing migration system places

---

Filling in the gaps

relatively little pressure on our ability to judge and forecast skills shortages, introducing a new system that allows far less easy access to migrant labour will require further investment in understanding what skills the UK labour market needs. Furthermore such a system will have to cover a far larger proportion of the labour market than it does currently; the majority of EU migrants work in occupations in the top half of the skills distribution and so a more controlled system could involve managing the labour market on an unprecedented scale.[9]

At present the majority of skilled (non-EU/EEA) migrants come to work in the UK through the Tier 2 visa route. Of these, two-thirds come on an intra-company transfer (ICT). The next most common route is when a firm proves that a UK resident can't do the job (satisfying the Resident Labour Market Test (RLMT)). Finally, fewer than 10,000 people enter each year through the shortage occupation list.

The body that currently advises government in navigating these challenges is the Migration Advisory Committee (MAC) and its role will need to be significantly expanded going forward. It is welcome that the government has already showed some recognition of this need. At present the MAC assesses if an occupation should go on the shortage list for occupations where Tier 2 visas are available. Given that the majority of EU migrants work in skilled occupations this route is likely to have to play a much more significant role in a post-Brexit system, where it covers EU/EEA migrants. Smaller firms in particular who do not have access to ICTs for skilled labour will need to look to this route. Fewer than 10,000 visas are awarded through the shortage occupation list each year and annually around 150,000 EU migrants come to the UK to work. Therefore it is possible that the shortage occupation list, and other skilled immigration routes, will have to be significantly expanded. Reassessing which occupations are likely to be on an expanded shortage occupation list (something we discuss in more detail in the next chapter), or how sectors are going to access the skills they need through other routes, once we leave the EU will be a significant task for the government and the MAC.

> Less than one in ten firms expect a salary threshold to apply to EU/EEA migrants in future

If migration falls over the long-term, the MAC, may also need to have an expanded remit to assess not just short term shortages but the extent to which UK workers can be trained to fill skill shortages in future, in which sectors businesses may be able to substitute machines for labour, and ultimately which industries will be reliant on migrant labour indefinitely. Such a task will be a big departure from the MAC's current role, and would clearly require wider work with parts of government, but would be necessary if net migration is to be significantly reduced without depriving firms – that may not be able to change the way they operate – of the labour they need.

To reinforce wider changes that will be required beyond simply applying our existing non-EU migration system to labour from the EU is the fact that less than one in ten firms expect a salary threshold to apply to EU/EEA migrants in future, yet the current system for non-EU/EEA migrants is based on such a threshold. The current regime restricts non-EU/EEA migration to workers that earn at least £30,000 (often the threshold is higher) and only medical radiographers, nurses, paramedics or secondary school teacher in some subjects are allowed to earn less. In contrast currently around 27,000 migrants work in high-skilled occupations (those in which over half of people have a degree) but earn less than £30,000 a year. Three quarters of these work in the following seven occupations:

At present employing non-EU/EEA migrants is expensive and complex

- **Teaching and Educational Professionals**
- **Nursing and Midwifery Professionals**
- **Business, Research and Administrative Professionals**
- **IT and Telecommunications Professionals**
- **Administrative Occupations: Records**
- **Health Professionals**
- **Public Services and Other Associate Professionals**

It is likely that many of the occupations above (aside from those which already benefit from salary exemptions) will require salary exemptions in future.

At present employing non-EU/EEA migrants is expensive and complex. Even small firms are required to pay a minimum of £2,000 to employ someone for the first year and £1,000 a year after that.[10] Costs rise if someone needs to be hired at short notice, and the government has made it clear that charges will rise significantly in future. This also doesn't take into account the significant costs associated with navigating the system. The Institute of Directors claims that due to cost and complexity small firms find it difficult to hire foreign workers.[11] Running the system is also expensive for the exchequer and expanding it will require significant investment.

One way to minimise both the cost to business and to the government described above would be to have a simpler, although less controlled immigration system for EU/EEA migrants. Two suggestions that have been proposed would be to make EU/EEA nationals who wanted to work in the UK apply for a visa through a similar system to that for non-EU/EEA nationals but one with lower thresholds (in terms of earnings, qualifications, etc). Another approach would be to impose no restrictions on EU/EEA nationals but cap the number that can come here to work on monthly or annual basis.[12] We suggest a different proposal; to permit migration by EU/EEA migrants with a job offer in an occupation on the shortage list. To minimise costs this regime should make it as easy to hire needed skilled EU migrants as possible. This would satisfy firms operating in areas where experts have concluded there is a genuine shortage, and could be combined with MAC recommended time limits (perhaps dictated by the time expected to train UK workers to fill the roles or for less labour intensive ways of working to be introduced).

Short-term, relatively low-skilled immigration

It is a fallacy that migrants can be neatly categorised into either high or low skilled. Even amongst EU2 and EU8 migrants 30 – 40 per cent are in occupations in the top half of the skills distribution.[13] Nevertheless there are some sectors that are reliant on relatively short-term, low-skilled migration. Furthermore every year at least as many, if not twice as many, short-term EU migrants come to the UK as long-term ones.[14] As we outlined in the introduction this is the part of our labour market where the increased costs of labour are likely to most acutely interact with shifts in labour supply via migration changes.

The UK used to run seasonal workers schemes, in particular the Seasonal Agricultural Workers Scheme (SAWS), the Sector Based Scheme (SBS) and the Tier 3 route for unskilled migrants. However the first two were discontinued and the last never used because it was felt that the supply of labour from the EU/EEA was sufficient. David Metcalfe, the previous head of the MAC, has already suggested that a temporary worker scheme could be restarted for low skilled migrants post-Brexit.

Other countries operate such schemes with a number of common features; employers

Figure 3: **Agricultural firms are most likely to be satisfied with a temporary worker scheme**

Proportion of firms that want a system where EU/EEA nationals coming to work are only allowed to stay for a certain period of time

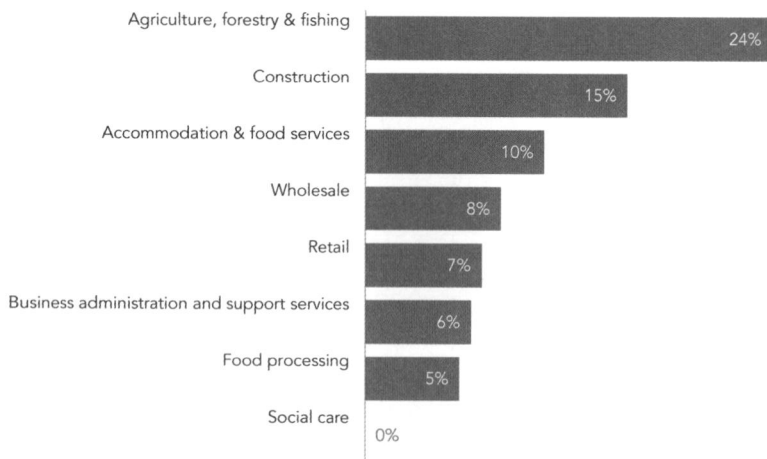

Base: All business decision-makers employing EU/EEA nationals (n=503)

Work in Brexit Britain

needing to prove that natives cannot do the work, employers paying a charge to employ migrants and being responsible for ensuring their departure. In some cases employers even need to prove that employing a migrant will not adversely affect the wages or

---

i Box 3: The agricultural sector

Different sectors will respond in very different ways to shifts in migration. Agriculture is a sector that – at least for some products – employs a lot of migrants for short time periods and has experience of using temporary worker schemes. We conducted interviews with employers to understand if the referendum had had any effect on recruitment, how they planned to react to any staffing problems in future and what immigration system would be best for their sector.

All interviewees have experienced difficulties recruiting EU staff since the referendum. Compared to 18 months ago one employer had seen the numbers of prospective staff decline from around 800 to 50. This was interpreted as being both due to the fall in the value of the pound since June 2016 and the uncertain long-term position of EU nationals in the UK. Employers have reacted to this by increasing investment on advertising and recruitment in Romania and Bulgaria.

Each interviewee spoke of their desire to use more robots but the required technology was thought to be 10 years or so away from market. As a result of the seasonal and relatively low-paid nature of the work, alongside a tight labour market and the fact that many are located in rural areas, the firms felt that it was unlikely that British workers could fill the emerging gaps. They argued that the wage hike required to make the seasonal roles attractive to British workers would make the business unprofitable.

Most interviewees viewed a return to the Seasonal Agricultural Workers Scheme as an acceptable alternative to free movement, which remained their preference. However, for non-seasonal parts of the sector, such as brassica, a seasonal scheme would not be appropriate and they face similar challenges to other sectors that employ large proportions of migrants. An income or skills-based scheme was not favoured by the businesses we interviewed. They pointed to the fact that the horticultural sector alone requires 80 thousand seasonal workers each year.[15] Without access to migrant labour the interviewees said the remaining options available were to greatly reduce output, move operations abroad or wind up the business.

---

employment prospects for natives. It has been suggested that more sectors (other than just agriculture and food manufacturing) could make use of such schemes once we leave the EU. However, this could be a very challenging task. Such temporary schemes suit agriculture, with its reliance on temporary labour and history of using gangmasters and other intermediaries to recruit, house and manage migrants, but would be difficult for other sectors without these features, or history of using such temporary worker schemes.

Our polling (Figure 3) showed that agricultural firms are most likely to be in favour of such a system (see Box 3), perhaps unsurprising given that they have benefitted from one in the past. However it is noticeable that, in general, support for such a scheme is tepid at best, again indicating the disconnect between the migrant labour regime firms may face and what they hope for. Once again such a system will require evidence based decisions about which lower-paying sectors could have access to this route and for what time period, something government is not currently set up for. Inevitably significant lobbying around which sectors are covered can be expected, this increases the need for a clear lead on recommendations to come from a strong, independent institution like the MAC.

A new migration regime needs to address the stock as well as the flow of migrant labour

Although a lot of attention has been directed at what immigration system may supersede the current one, perhaps more important for the UK labour market is to reassure and guarantee the rights of those migrants living and working in the UK at the moment. If such reassurance is not provided, and emigration increases, then labour shortages are likely to be far more damaging given the reliance of many firms on these workers.

Providing such guarantees is no simple task – the Institute for Government estimates that this may take many years or the hiring of an additional 5,000 civil servants to process the permanent residence claims – however until this is done it will not be possible to introduce any new immigration system given the importance of being able to distinguish recently-arrived EU migrants from those that have been here for some time.[16]

A proactive approach should lead to a better understanding of the skills and investment needs of the UK labour market

A renewed focus on enforcement will be needed

A new immigration system is likely to increase the need for significant investment in labour market enforcement, to ease the transition and ensure that migrants – many of whom will have different rights depending on their exact migration status – have their rights respected. Once the new system is in place the need for greater levels of enforcement will remain, both to ensure a level playing field for businesses and to avoid

> ## *i* Box 4: Regional immigration systems
>
> Other countries, notably Australia and Canada, have a regional element to their immigration systems and there has been some discussion of having something similar in the UK.[17] Our survey shows that what firms want does differ by region. For example approximately 56 per cent of Scottish firms polled want to keep freedom of movement compared to 24 per cent in the West Midlands. However the Home Office has stated that it is not considering a regional approach to migration, such a regional system would require further investment, particularly in enforcement. It would also require political support, something hindered by a lack of regional political structures in much of England.

exploitation. While the migration debate includes lots of references to the border, given that we are unlikely to start requiring EU/EEA visitors to the UK to apply for visas it is likely that it will be the labour market that is the point of enforcement in reality.

In that context it is welcome that David Metcalf was recently appointed to be the first Director of Labour Market Enforcement, overseeing the three bodies with a role in enforcement of labour market standards and regulations (HMRC, Gangmasters and Labour Abuse Authority and the Employment Agency Standards Inspectorate). In the future these bodies will have to oversee significantly more migrants with constraints on their right to work in the UK and so there will need to be significantly more investment to ensure that labour market standards are enforced and that people do not overstay their visas. At the moment the Home Office grants around 160,000 working visas to people from outside the EU/EEA and their dependents per year and spends £427 million on enforcement. Based on long and short-term migration data we know that around 150,000 EU/EEA migrants come to the UK to work per year. In the future these people will require visas and they will need to leave the country once their visas expire. The enforcement budget will have to be significantly expanded, if not doubled.

Taking back control on migration requires a clearer vision for what the country's immigration policy is trying to achieve

Putting in place a new system and helping firms and the labour market adjust to it requires a clearer sense of what we want the immigration system to achieve. One of the big impacts of Brexit is that we are - to a great extent - able to take decisions about our approach to migration. But doing so requires government owning the trade-offs inherent in any migration policy. Should firms be able to easily get the labour they need to grow in all cases? Are there types of output we are happy to see stop being produced in the UK if that is the price of lower migration? How do we encourage firms to invest in skills and technology, without them facing short term skills shortages?

Taking back control means the UK government will need to answer these questions in a way it hasn't for a generation, and in a way that brings together immigration policy with wider labour market decision making. Reinforcing the sense that there are many more questions to be answered, the Conservative manifesto stated that the party will help sectors suffering skills shortages and support those that are 'strategically important'. Aligning the system with the industrial strategy is a good idea but the devil will be in the detail, not least which sectors are deemed to be strategically important and by whom. Similarly the Labour party have made it clear that economic need will inform any future immigration system and recognises that many sectors depend on migrant labour, again though more detail is needed.

It is not just government that needs that vision as a guide, it is also a matter of urgency given the very worrying complacency of many firms, many of whom believe that the world is going to continue as it currently does with very little change impacting on them. In place of that lack of preparedness for change we need business to have the clarity that allows long term decisions on investment, training and indeed what they produce to be taken. There may be a temptation to delay a decision on the shape of an intended migration system given the wish for leverage in the Brexit negotiations, however the strategic needs of the UK labour market are more important than such tactical considerations. Furthermore a proactive approach should lead to a better understanding of the skills and investment needs of the UK labour market at a time when costs are rising and supply is likely to shrink at the bottom of the labour market. It is to this that the next chapter turns.

Summary of recommendations

— Skills

Recommendation 1 **The MAC should have a greater role, and additional resources, to inform decision making on the UK's skills needs and migration.**

Recommendation 2 **More occupations will probably need an exemption from the current salary threshold for skilled migration.**

— Costs

Recommendation 3 **We can minimise the costs of any new immigration system by allowing migration by EU/EEA nationals with a job offer in a shortage occupation.**

Recommendation 4 **New temporary worker schemes will have to be created and, for those sectors that have no experience of using these, support should be provided.**

— Enforcement

Recommendation 5 **The Home Office's enforcement budget may need to rise from £427 million to as much as double this.**

— Rights

Recommendation 6 **Need to guarantee the rights of those migrants that currently live and work in the UK given how much the UK labour market depends on them.**

— Next steps

Recommendation 7 **In the near future the new government should publish a green paper setting out its vision for what the new immigration system aims to achieve by the end of 2017.**

Filling in the gaps

ComRes interviewed 503 business decision makers employing EU/EEA workers online between 12th and 26th April 2017. Data were weighted to be demographically representative of GB businesses by number of employees.

1 We define migrants as those not born in the UK.

2 RF analysis of ONS, *LFS*

3 HM Government, *The United Kingdom's exit from and new partnership with the European Union*, February 2017

4 J Owen, *Implementing Brexit: Immigration*, Institute for Government, May 2017

5 The Observer, "Record numbers of EU nurses quit NHS", 18 March 2017; The Guardian, "Farmers deliver stark warning over access to EU seasonal workers", 21 February 2017.

6 KPMG, *Labour migration in the hospitality sector*, March 2017

7 Resolution Foundation survey by ComRes, fieldwork 12th - 26th April 2017

8 The EU-Canada Comprehensive Economic and Trade Agreement (CETA) includes provisions making it easier for companies to transfer employees between the EU and Canada and provisions making it easier for EU professionals to temporarily supply certain services in Canada.

9 Office for National Statistics, International immigration and the labour market, UK: 2016, April 2016

10 Fees and charges include: Visa application fee (£575), standard visa processing fee (£150), Sponsorship Licence (£536 per annum), Certification of sponsorship (£199), Immigration skills charge (£364 per annum), NHS Levy (in theory paid by an employee but charged at the time of application - £200 per annum)

11 S Nevin, *Brexit: UK–EU movement of people – oral evidence*, EU Home Affairs Sub-Committee, 2017

12 J Portes, "Immigration – the way forward", in Brexit Beckons: *Thinking ahead by leading economists*, VoxEU, August 2016

13 Office for National Statistics, *International immigration and the labour market, UK: 2016*, April 2016

14 Office for National Statistics, *Note on the difference between National Insurance number registrations and the estimate of long-term international migration: 2016*, May 2016

15 NFU, *NFU welcomes seasonal labour debate*, November 2016

16 J Owen, *Implementing Brexit: Immigration*, Institute for Government, May 2017

17 All Party Parliamentary Group on Social Integration, *Interim Report into the Integration of Immigrants*, January 2017

Work in Brexit Britain

CHAPTER THREE

A firm response

Business responses to the labour market
tipping point will vary by sector

Kathleen Henehan

The state we're in

Automation provides a route for some sectors, including construction and retail, to adjust to a changing labour market

But UK total investment is currently lower than the OECD and European Union averages

The occupations facing skills shortages could double, providing a further spur to change in some sectors

The proportion of adults with access to work-based training is below the OECD average and most training lasts less than a week

What should we do?

As part of an industrial strategy the government should proactively make sectoral deals with those industries most affected by changes at the bottom of the labour market – particularly those likely to struggle with automation or face severe skills shortages

The government should do more to encourage firms to make use of apprenticeships of Level 3 and above and more apprenticeships should come with nationally recognised qualifications

So far we have set out significant changes that are likely to affect the bottom of the UK labour market in the coming years, and the difficulty firms may have responding to those changes if they are unprepared for them – as they currently are on migration. The next question centres on what types of responses are feasible and desirable, once the reality of change has been recognised. Chapters 4-6 explore the role that government can play in responding to and shaping this changing labour market, but the subject of this chapter is the response we might expect from firms themselves.

In particular, we note that among the firms and sectors most affected by the tipping point of the availability and relative price of lower paid labour, very different adjustment strategies will be relevant. For some, the prospect of automation, far from being the job-destroying bogeyman of much media coverage, may provide a viable adjustment strategy to a higher productivity business model. This chapter identifies where that may be the case, however it notes the worrying trend that many industries with the most to gain from increases in investment have traditionally been among the least likely to engage in such activity.

For other firms affected by labour market shifts, the nature of the work and state of technology means such an approach may not be viable. This is particularly concerning in sectors that also look likely to face the most severe skills shortages. These sections of our economy should be a key part of any industrial strategy because of the clear need for a shared view of their future role in the UK economy between firms and government. Changing what they produce as well as how it is produced will be important questions going forward.

Understanding how responses to the tipping point might vary across the UK economy – and therefore where the biggest challenges may be – will be crucial to making sure the country is as prepared as it can be for the change that is underway.

Some lower skilled sectors could make significant gains from increased automation, but investment levels are low

Economic theory, international evidence and some early indications from firms' response to the rising National Living Wage (NLW) point to greater investment in capital being a key route through which firms respond to a combination of rising labour costs at the bottom end of the labour market and tightened labour supply. The financial incentives to do so clearly rise with labour costs, while tight and very uncertain labour supply prospects will also make the case for greater investment in capital.

> Not all firms and sectors have the same opportunities for technology-linked productivity gains

International evidence on how businesses respond to big reductions in low-paid migration does show significant shifts towards more automation (alongside changes in what is produced in the first place).[1] Domestically, this is also a message that has come through in our research, with two in three firms affected by the NLW for example taking up measures in the first six months to increase their productivity.[2] Encouragingly, a third of firms we surveyed who felt that a fall in EU migration would lead them to change the way their business is run said that they would invest more in technology.[3] Such an approach would be the reverse of one explanation for why the post-crisis fall in productivity (the so-called productivity puzzle) has been particularly deep for the UK, where the argument runs that firms have substituted relatively cheap and available labour for investment in capital.[4]

However, while there is clearly appetite among some firms, the extent to which capital investment and greater automation is a feasible response will vary hugely. Simply put, not all firms and sectors have the same opportunities for technology-linked productivity gains.

A firm response

To assess which sectors most affected by coming shifts to the low-paid part of the UK labour market have the greatest potential to respond with greater automation, we can use work showing the number of jobs that could be replaced by robots over the coming years. These estimates – which vary from 10 per cent to 35 per cent of jobs by the early 2030s – are inevitably highly uncertain and are more typically set out as describing the scale of the 'threat' posed by robots to existing workers.[5] However, the estimates might also be considered to show the scale of 'opportunity' for automation that exists across different industries. They provide a useful jumping off point for considering where across the UK economy automation looks most and least likely to occur. In this chapter we use the estimates produced by Bakhshi, Frey and Osborne, which given they suggest more scope for automation than some of the other estimates can perhaps be thought of as an upper-limit to what we can expect from sectors.

Figure 1 sets out the results. Among the sectors most likely to be affected by the labour market shifts underpinning this book big differences are visible, with the agricultural sector having the most significant scope for further automation and social care having very little at all.

Figure 1: **Automation**

Probability of automation (>1 is above average)

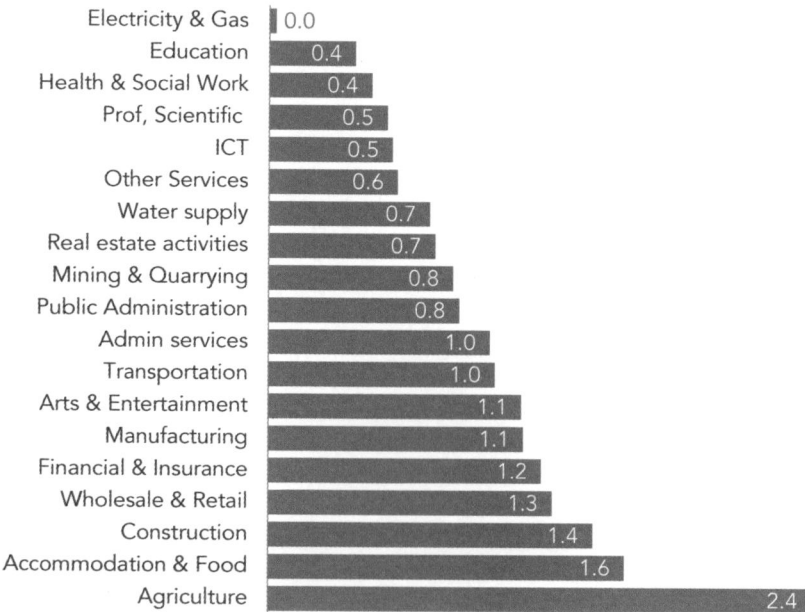

Electricity & Gas	0.0
Education	0.4
Health & Social Work	0.4
Prof, Scientific	0.5
ICT	0.5
Other Services	0.6
Water supply	0.7
Real estate activities	0.7
Mining & Quarrying	0.8
Public Administration	0.8
Admin services	1.0
Transportation	1.0
Arts & Entertainment	1.1
Manufacturing	1.1
Financial & Insurance	1.2
Wholesale & Retail	1.3
Construction	1.4
Accommodation & Food	1.6
Agriculture	2.4

Source: RF analysis of Bakhshi et al, 2015

Drilling down below the broad industrial categories depicted in the chart, we can isolate those sectors that are judged as having a relatively high probability of automation (within the top 25 of the 80 sectors) and are most affected by higher costs and lower availability of low paid labour. We are left with a list of 11 industries that could be particularly affected by rising labour costs and reduced access to migrant labour (see Chapter 2), and which might be well placed to make gains via automation:

- Agriculture
- Food and drink service activities
- Postal and courier activities
- Retail trade
- Gambling and betting activities
- Printing and recorded media
- Specialised construction (electrical work, demolition, plumbing)
- Accommodation
- Construction of buildings
- Manufacturing of materials (metal, paper, plastic, textiles)
- Food manufacturing

The history of investment in the UK offers some caution about whether these opportunities for automation will be realised

The fact that opportunities for investment in technology exist for firms considering responses to a changing labour market is, however, only part of the answer. Firms also have to take advantage of those opportunities.

It is therefore not encouraging that UK capital investment is low by international standards. Gross fixed capital formation is lower than the OECD and Euro Area averages and firms account for a smaller share of total British investment than in many other developed countries.[6]

Moving beyond the overall poor investment performance, sectoral level analysis reinforces the scale of the change in business models and behaviour that a shift towards capital investment in low paying sectors would mean. Figure 2 compares the estimated propensity for automation across sectors (x-axis), with changes in investment levels between 1997 and 2015 (y-axis).

> It is not encouraging that UK capital investment is low by international standards

The first thing to note is investment in machinery and intellectual property has fallen in many sectors, further emphasising that there may be a general dearth of investment. Secondly there has been no strong evidence that investment over the last 20 years has been any higher among these lower-paid, more tech-ready industries. There are exceptions to this (agriculture) but the general picture is that some sectors have taken advantage of technology (finance) whereas other sectors have remained labour intensive, including those that we are now focused on (construction and retail for example). Although there are some sectors that buck the trend (health and social work stand out) the wider evidence is that even in low-paying sectors where technology is available, investment is lower than is recorded in the same sectors in other European countries.[7]

Even where the opportunity for greater automation exists, it will of course be for firms in such sectors to decide themselves whether or not the tipping point associated

Figure 2: **Automation and investment across UK industries**

Change in machinery and IP investment per worker (1997 - 2015)

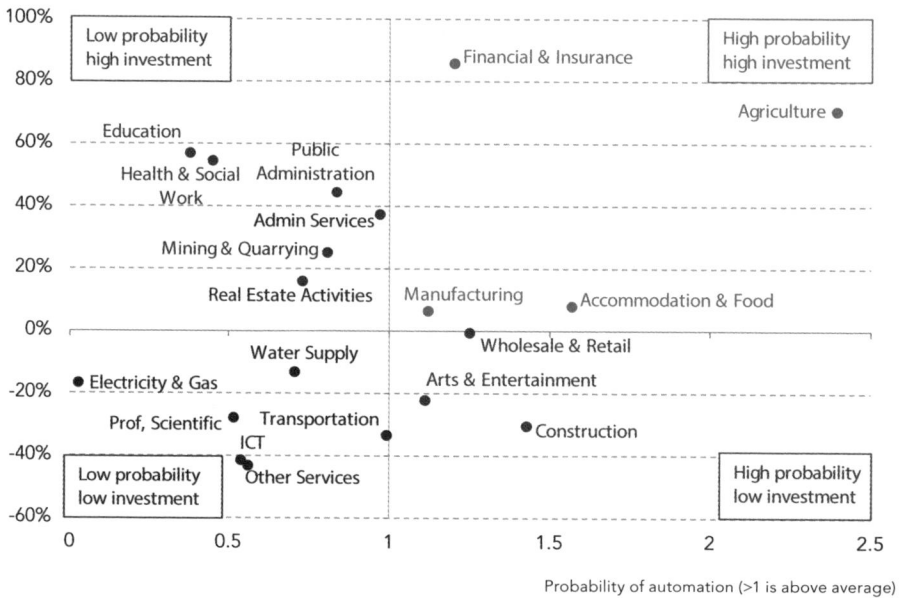

Probability of automation (>1 is above average)

Sources: RF analysis of Bakhshi et al, 2015, & ONS, *LFS*

with changes at the bottom end of the labour market is sufficient to spur them into action. In all likelihood, normal market forces will dictate that some firms react and progress, while others struggle to adapt.

Much bigger will be the challenge facing firms in sectors where technology has less obvious applications, particularly where this coincides with potential labour shortages associated with lower migration. It is to this issue that we now turn.

The scale of challenge in different sectors will also be affected by skills shortages that changes in migration create

Alongside investment in technology, adjusting their use of human capital is a key part of the response available to firms. Even ahead of the Brexit vote, UK firms voiced concern over their access to the skills they need. In 2015, businesses reported over 200,000 skill shortage vacancies, up 43 per cent on 2013.[8] Likewise, in April 2016 – just ahead of the referendum – nearly 70 per cent of firms (a record high) told the Confederation of Business Industry that they couldn't access enough workers with the skills they needed.[9]

As discussed in Chapters 1 and 2, the process of Brexit and any associated reduction in the supply of foreign labour is likely to compound this problem, particularly in the short term. Hiring workers from EU/EEA countries is currently relatively straight-forward, in contrast to the complexity involved with recruiting workers from the rest of the world to fill skills shortages. We discussed the UK's immigration system and the role of the Migration Advisory Council (MAC) at length in the previous chapter, but the focus here is on one particular part of the system, the shortage occupation list, and what it can tell us about where firms' might struggle most to respond to a changing labour market.

i Box 1: How the MAC decides if an occupation should go on the shortage list

The MAC provides advice to the government on which skilled occupations (non-skilled are not considered) should be placed on the shortage list.[10] It conducts analysis using a variety of indicators of labour market shortage. These are split into four types:
- employer-based (surveys about demand for workers and vacancies);
- price-based (market pressure on wages);
- volume-based (utilisation indicators, such as rises in hours worked or employment levels); and
- indicators of imbalance (such as vacancy duration or claimant count by sought occupation).

The MAC also makes a 'bottom-up' assessment of occupations by speaking to professionals and sectoral representatives. It only decides to place an occupation on the list if it believes that bringing in immigrants would have little detrimental impact on local skills acquisition, productivity, and the wider UK labour market. [11]

A firm response

In order to explore which occupations are more likely to face skills shortages in the new world of an end to free movement, we – as far as possible – can replicate the MAC's approach.[12] In our simplified thought experiment, we remove all EU/EEA migrants from the workforce and consider how different occupations then fare against the MAC scoring system. This is of course an extreme example, but serves as a useful illustration of the sectors which might face additional skill shortages under a tighter post-Brexit migration regime.

In total, 50 out of 369 occupations (14 per cent) are flagged as facing shortages in our model – almost double the current number of occupations on the MAC list. Figure 3 sets out these occupations and splits them on the basis of underlying skill level (y-axis) and average pay (x-axis). These distinctions matter because, although we have no indication yet from the government about how they intend to address skills shortages within a new migration regime, lower-skilled occupations are less likely to make it onto any future MAC shortage list, while occupations with lower pay rates are likely to find it harder to entice UK workers to plug any gaps, and firms in these areas will also face the challenge of responding to a higher NLW.

Figure 3: **Sectors that may face skills shortages after freedom of movement ends**

Share of people with a degree in the occupation

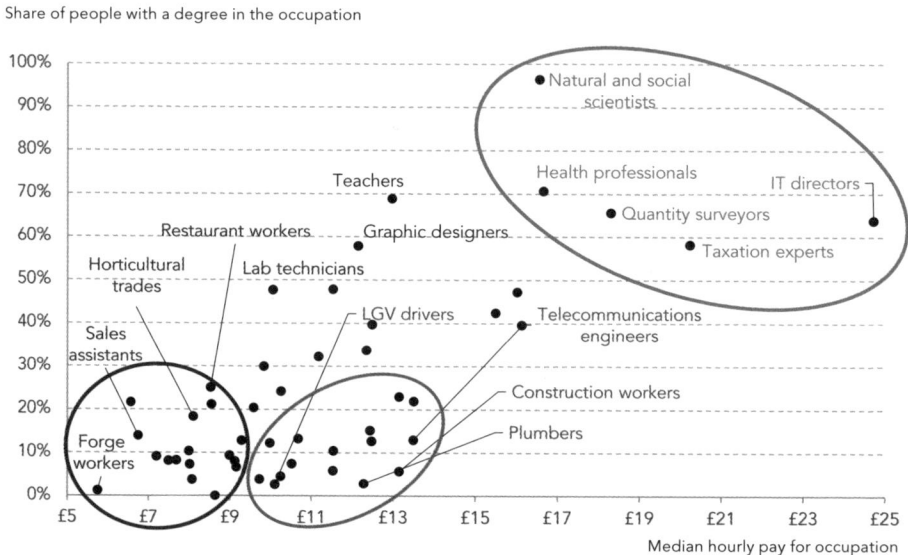

Median hourly pay for occupation

Notes: Wage data is from the Labour Force Survey. This is less accurate than sources such as the Annual Survey of Hours and Earnings (ASHE), but allows us to look at pay by occupation and education.

Source: RF analysis of ONS, *LFS*

Work in Brexit Britain

We can identify three different groups of occupations from this chart. Largely irrelevant to the focus of this piece are those in the top right that are both relatively high-skilled and relatively high-paying. They are therefore more likely to qualify for the shortage list (indeed some are already on the list) and meet the salary threshold. As noted in the last chapter though, some slightly lower-paying but higher-skilled occupations – such as teachers and graphic designers – might face more difficulties given the current level of the salary threshold.

Shifting to a second group in the bottom centre part of the chart – covering occupations such as plumbers, construction workers, telecom engineers and technicians – we might speculate that firms relying on these occupations are unlikely to benefit from access to labour from the current non-EU/EEA migration regime. That means a higher bar for a successful response to a shifting labour market. These firms do however have scope within existing business models to train up native workers to fill such roles, even if that has cost implications and requires a mindset change about who the firms' workers of tomorrow will be. Crucially, these occupations have pay levels above the NLW and so can offer pay progression to workers engaging in that training who would previously have been doing lower paid work.

> Encouragingly, employers are aware that human as well as physical capital change may be needed

In contrast, those sectors in the bottom left of the chart – including sales assistants, restaurant workers and LGV drivers – might be considered especially vulnerable as under current rules they are unlikely to qualify for the shortage list, face wider constraints on their ability to respond by spending on training or to compete on relative pay given they are most affected by the fast rising NLW. As we noted above, there might be some scope for automation, but this is not always the case. Where it is not, wider business model shifts will have to be examined, including lowering staff numbers (with quality effects), hiring workers from groups not previously looked to (including the young and disabled), or trying to move to a higher-paying equilibrium to attract staff with obvious implications for prices and profits. Some firms could also decide to stop producing certain goods and services in the UK.

Adjusting to greater investment in human capital will not be straightforward

By highlighting which sectors may face the most acute skills shortages or the least opportunity to look to automation, we can start to identify where firms relying on lower paid labour may have more difficulty adjusting to a changed labour market and where a focus on training might be most needed.

Encouragingly, employers are aware that human as well as physical capital change may be needed. In the survey of employers we carried out as part of this project, 34 per cent of firms said that, faced with a decline in EU labour, they would try to hire more British workers. Similarly, the most popular way that firms had attempted to raise productivity in response to the NLW was to invest in training.[13] Such initial steps are welcome and the government can stimulate further change by providing more clarity about how the future migration regime might operate, and in particular how skill shortages will be dealt with.

The worrying news for our post-Brexit world of work is that – despite positive intentions – British firms tend to underinvest in human capital. The proportion of adults with access to work-based training is below the OECD average, and most training (52 per cent) lasts less than a week.[14] More generally, business surveys indicate the need to upskill and retrain workers of all ages and qualification levels.[15]

Perhaps more troublingly in the context of how well our skills system is set-up to ease the load of firms responding to shifts at the bottom of the labour market, UK skills training is unequally distributed. It tends to be undertaken primarily by those with higher qualifications and higher pay. This is perhaps unsurprising and is partly explained by the fact that training tends to raise wages. However, it does suggest that those sectors that may be in most need of additional investment in human capital in the future are the least likely to get it.

The problem is compounded by the fact that the 60 per cent of young people who do not go onto university at age 18 face a bewildering array of educational pathways. These often do a poor job of equipping them with the skills necessary for the modern labour market.[16] In short, education and training may be able to address some of the skills shortages that the UK is likely to face in future. But this will not happen until technical education and work-based training are actively improved.

Supporting firms contending with a labour market tipping point means improving the domestic skills system

In large part it will be for firms themselves to determine the most appropriate response to the pressures associated with the combination of rising costs in the bottom part of the labour market and an exogenous labour supply shock. Alongside the efforts we have set out above that are designed to maintain a certain level of output, it's also feasible that firms decide to trade down on quality or simply produce less.

Ultimately we can expect market forces to bring UK businesses to a new equilibrium in the post-Brexit world. But government intervention could help both ease the transition to this new equilibrium and nudge it in the direction of a higher-value economic model.

By way of preparing for the end of free movement, the MAC should undertake a similar exercise to the one we have set out above – providing an assessment of the occupations it expects to be most affected. Once it does this, the government will be in a better place to provide guidance to firms about whether they can expect to access migrant labour once the country leaves the EU. Some expansion of the shortage occupation list – given the potential doubling in our modelling – is likely to be necessary. But it is important that the government provides more clarity about which occupations are unlikely to make the list. The more detail firms have, the more likely they are to make investment decisions that take a number of years to come to fruition.

The new Apprenticeship Levy is another opportunity to increase technical skills provision

There should also be a wider evaluation of how the new immigration system interacts with the UK's skills system (something we discussed in more detail in the previous chapter). This is particularly important given that a significant expansion of the shortage occupation list may run against the government's target of reducing net migration to the tens of thousands.

Improving the UK skills system – especially in relation to intermediate skills and technical education – is a big task, and one worth undertaking even in the absence of any shift in the functioning of our labour market.[17] For example, there should be more intermediate and higher-level technical provision. The Government's Post-16 Skills Plan and the Apprenticeship Levy provide an opportunity to do this.

The Post-16 Skills Plan set out welcome plans to streamline technical education options for 16-19 year-olds by providing 15 new technical education routes, called 'T-Levels'.[18] Average annual teaching hours on these courses will rise to 900, up from the 600 currently provided to this age group. In order to get these programmes right, extra teaching will require additional funding.

In the 2017 Spring Budget the Chancellor committed additional annual funding allocations of between £115 and £445m, as each of the courses are rolled out. In their 2017 manifesto, the Labour Party similarly proposed a funding increase, by bringing all 16-18 year old programmes in line with baseline funding for 14-16 year olds.

The new Apprenticeship Levy is another opportunity to increase technical skills provision, but there is a danger that expansion comes at the expense of quality. At present, 42 per cent of new apprenticeship standards are at Level 3 and in 2015/16, only 40 per cent of completed apprenticeships were at Level 3 or higher.[19] This should be helped to rise in future. In addition, more apprenticeships should offer a nationally recognised qualification; only around two-thirds do currently.

Importantly, an increased number of higher quality options will not have the desired effect unless people understand how to access them. The government needs to ensure that the push to have more apprenticeships does not produce a plethora of different standards which are difficult for prospective candidates to understand. Worryingly, there is some evidence that this is happening; there have been 172 new apprenticeship standards already approved and a further 218 are in development.

Those sectors facing the most difficult transition should be a priority for the new industrial strategy

This chapter has sketched out the kind of analysis that can start to inform a view about which sectors face the biggest challenges in adjusting to an era of less available and more expensive low paid labour. A recognition of those challenges would help the government refocus its forthcoming industrial strategy on these big shifts at the bottom of the UK labour market.

The draft industrial strategy offers to adopt a sectoral approach with those sectors that choose to come together and ask for one. A more proactive approach would see government identifying those sectors with the least straightforward responses to a changed labour market, be that because of limited scope for automation or the depth of skills shortages, and prioritising those sectors for engagement with the industrial strategy.

The industrial strategy is a good opportunity to ensure that a welcome overarching focus on productivity growth involves boosting output in both high-skill, high-value industries and lower-paid ones that are too often ignored in such visions but are set for the biggest labour market upheaval. Likewise, it would be wrong to place all the emphasis in this area on new technology, when the wider adoption of existing technology is also key. Although UK businesses outperform those in many other developed countries, management skills lag behind firms in countries such as the US, Japan, Germany and Canada,[20] meaning there are gains to be made from the sharing of best practice and a new focus on organisational capabilities.

This chapter has provided an indication of how different sectors may respond to a changing labour market. In the end, the success or otherwise of firms in adjusting to this new world will be shaped by market forces, but government has a role to play in providing guidance as to what the UK's immigration and skills systems will look like in the future and in proactively helping workers and firms adjust to the changes. One area where more action is needed – increasing engagement with the labour market – is the focus of the next chapter.

Summary of recommendations

— Immigration and skills

Recommendation 1 **The government should commission the MAC to model the impact that the end of free movement will have on different sectors and occupations**

Recommendation 2 **The government will probably have to enlarge the shortage occupation list – perhaps almost doubling the number of occupations – but it should make it clear which occupations will move onto the shortage list once freedom of movement ends**

— The domestic skills system

Recommendation 3 **The government should incentivise firms to make use of apprenticeships at Level three and above**

Recommendation 4 **More apprenticeships should offer a nationally recognised qualification**

Recommendation 5 **The government should ensure that apprenticeship standards do not proliferate to the point where they are confusing for firms and prospective apprentices**

— Industrial strategy

Recommendation 6 **The government should proactively approach those sectors that will be most affected by the end of freedom of movement and rising labour costs as part of its industrial strategy rather than waiting for sectors to come forward.**

A firm response

1 M A Clemens, E G Lewis & H M Postel, "Immigration restrictions as active labour market policy: evidence from the Mexican Bracero Exclusion", *NBER Working Paper 23125*, February 2017

2 C D'Arcy, *Industrial strategies? Exploring responses to the National Living Wage in low-paying sectors*, Resolution Foundation for the Low Pay Commission, December 2016

3 Resolution Foundation survey by ComRes, fieldwork 12th - 26th April 2017

4 J Pessoa & J Van Reenen, "The UK Productivity and Jobs Puzzle: Does the Answer Lie in Labour Market Flexibility?", *LSE Centre for Economic Performance Special Paper* No. 31, June 2013

5 PWC, *Consumer spending prospects and the impact of automation on jobs UK Economic Outlook*, March 2017 "Haldane (2015) cites a Bank of England estimate of around this level for the UK based on their version of the Frey and Osborne analysis. This is also in line with other estimates by Frey and Osborne themselves for the UK"

6 RF analysis of OECD and World Bank data

7 S. Thompson et al., *Boosting Britain's Low-Wage Sectors: a Strategy for Productivity and Growth*, Institute for Public Policy Research, 2016.

8 UK Commission on Employment and Skills, *UKCES Employer Skills Survey 2015*: UK report, January 2016

9 Confederation of British Industry, *The right combination: CBI/Pearson Education and Skills Survey 2016*, July 2016

10 The MAC considers a 'skilled' occupation those that are NQF6+ (graduate level) occupations, although there is no exact proportion of graduates needed in an occupation to make it skilled.

11 Migration Advisory Committee, *Skilled Shortage Sensible: Full review of the recommended shortage occupation lists for the UK and Scotland, a sunset clause and the creative occupations*, February 2013

12 Returns to occupation, claimant count and vacancy postings/unemployment by sought occupation. Testing our approach using current data, we find that our model provides similar results to the MAC's. At the moment, 32 occupations are on the shortage list including artists, actuaries, engineers and highly skilled chefs, and our model identified a majority of these as being in shortage. The fact we didn't identify all the existing shortage occupations likely owes to the fact that the MAC uses more than just its statistical model to identify shortage occupations (as described in Box 1).

13 C D'Arcy, *Industrial strategies? Exploring responses to the National Living Wage in low-paying sectors*, Resolution Foundation for the Low Pay Commission, December 2016

14 RF analysis of ONS, *LFS*

15 UK Commission on Employment and Skills, *UKCES Employer Skills Survey 2015*: UK report, January 2016

16 C D'Arcy & D Finch, *Finding your routes: Non-graduate pathways in the UK's labour market*, Resolution Foundation for the Social Mobility Commission, May 2016

17 K Henehan, *Using the Apprenticeship Levy to tackle the UK's post-16 education divide*, Resolution Foundation, April 2016

18 The 15 routes are scheduled to come online between 2019-20 and 2021-22

19 Department for Education, "Further Education and Skills," Table 7, March 2017

20 N Bloom et al, "Management Practices Across Firms and Countries", *Academy of Management Perspectives*, February 2011

CHAPTER FOUR

All working together

How to draw more people into the UK labour market

Stephen Clarke

The state we're in

Employment is at a record high of 75 per cent

Yet there is a 46 percentage point gap in participation rates between the best and worst performing groups in the labour market

Progress is possible: employment rates for single parents, the low qualified and older workers have risen significantly in the past two decades

What should we do?

Increase work allowances in Universal Credit for single parents and second earners to £2,000 and £1,500 respectively; restore work allowances for disabled recipients to value originally intended

Create a statutory 'right to return' period of one year for those absent from work due to sickness, coupled with a rebate on sick pay costs for firms

The government should explore allowing for the partial drawdown of the state pension, reinstating the option to take a lump sum, and supporting the expansion of partial drawdown options in private pensions

T he last chapter focused on how firms might react to the changes in the labour market and how this would vary by sector. Firms may deal with the relative change in the price of low-wage labour by substituting labour for machines or taking on fewer – though perhaps more well-trained – staff. However this may not be an option for all firms and the reduction in migrant labour will mean that they will have to deal with a general supply shock. But we should remember that in the medium term the domestic labour supply is far from fixed. Government has a key role in helping more people engage with the labour market to ease the transition firms – particularly at the lower-paying end of the labour market – face in a world of lower migration.

Whatever challenges the UK's economy continues to face a decade on from the financial crisis, there can be no doubt that its headline performance on employment has been remarkable. From a 2011 trough, the number of people in work has jumped by more than two million, with the 16-64 employment rate seeming to reach new highs on an almost monthly basis.

Even before the Brexit vote there was a strong case for focusing on further increasing labour market participation in the UK, both as a key component of economic growth, a driver of highly progressive income rises and part of the answer to how we adjust to an ageing society. With the labour market tightening, and the prospect of lower net migration (and therefore labour supply) from the EU, doing so is now more of an imperative. This increasingly means bringing in workers from those groups that have traditionally been further away from the labour market, such as older people and those with health problems. That's not a straightforward task and one that is unlikely to be achieved without serious and sustained focus from government, but it is one at which the country has enjoyed some success before.

In this chapter we consider the lessons we can learn from past policy interventions and highlight those areas worth focusing on as we endeavour to push the country further towards full employment as part of an approach to successfully adjust to big shifts in our labour market.

Labour supply is tight, and getting tighter

Responding to our migration survey (discussed in Chapter 2), four in ten (38 per cent) firms that employ significant numbers of migrant workers said that they would hire more UK nationals if the supply of migrant labour fell after Brexit. Yet the employment rate among the UK-born population aged 16-64 is already 75.3 per cent. The unemployment rate for this group – which captures just those out-of-work individuals who are actively looking for a job – has returned to pre-crisis levels (Figure 1). Add in the fact that the working-age population is about to start shrinking as large numbers of the 'baby boomer' generation retire and the ease with which firms might draw in replacement staff without wider changes is clearly open to question.

Not all firms and sectors have obvious opportunities for technology-linked productivity gains

As we touched on in Chapter 2, one response to any reduction in the size of the workforce is to simply accept that we will produce less as a country. GDP would be lower but, to the extent that the population would also shrink, GDP per person might be sustained. However, this approach would have implications for our public finances (all else equal, the UK's stock of debt as a percentage of GDP would be higher if overall GDP was lower) and doesn't much help individual firms looking to maintain or increase output while wrestling with the challenges of a reduced availability of labour.

Figure 1: **Employment and unemployment for those born in the UK**

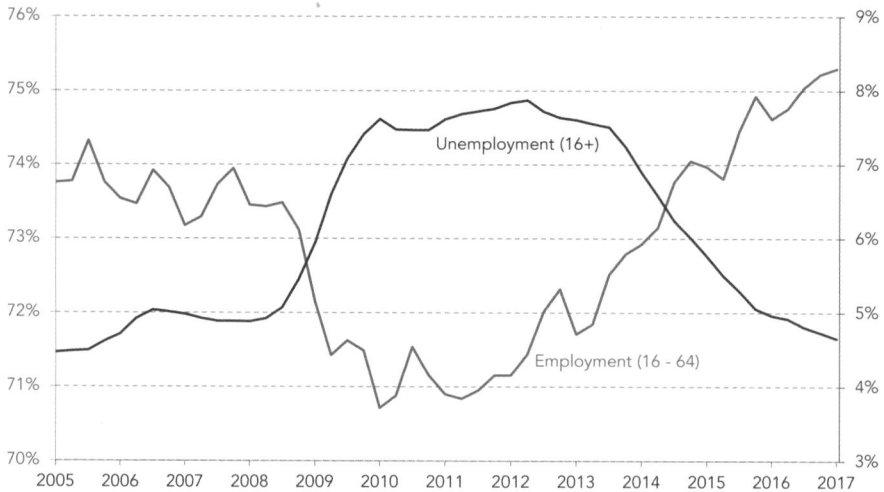

Source: RF analysis of ONS, *Labour Market Statistics*

However, the extent to which capital investment and greater automation is a feasible response will vary hugely across firms. Simply put, not all firms and sectors have obvious opportunities for technology-linked productivity gains.

Recognising the potential constraints on labour supply, 37 per cent of those firms saying they would recruit more UK nationals said that they would do so by expanding their pool of applicants. At the lower paying end of the labour market this in practice means looking to recruit workers from outside the current labour force. These firms will be helped by one of the big drivers of changes to this part of our labour market - the series of above-inflation increases in the wage floor associated with the development of the National Living Wage (NLW). Higher pay, particularly in this part of the wage distribution, should act as a pull factor by raising returns to work for many new entrants.

But experience tells us that market forces and wage incentives alone will prove insufficient to drive big structural increases in labour market participation. That is reinforced by evidence that employment levels vary significantly across the UK, but only a third of the gap between the best and worst performing areas can be attributed to differences in the functioning of the local economies.[1] A much larger part of the variation can instead be explained by differing levels of engagement across groups that we might label as 'low activity', such as older people, single parents, people with disabilities and ethnic minorities.

Boosting employment will increasingly rest on raising participation among 'low activity' groups

Figure 2 compares participation rates (that is, the proportion offering themselves up for work, irrespective of whether they are currently employed or not) within these 'low activity' groups with the 'high performer' group. This group – comprising white, non-single parent, highly qualified, non-disabled people – records a participation rate that is always and everywhere above 90 per cent. It appears relatively untouched by variation in either location or the economic cycle.

Three things are obvious from the chart. First, participation among most 'low activity' groups has improved substantially over the course of the 21st century so far, demonstrating that progress is possible. Secondly, all of these groups continue to lag well behind the 'high performer' group, highlighting the scope for improvement. Thirdly, recent experience has differed somewhat across the 'low activity' groups. The most dramatic improvements can be seen for single parents and older people whereas

Figure 2: 'Low-activity' groups have become more engaged with the labour market over time

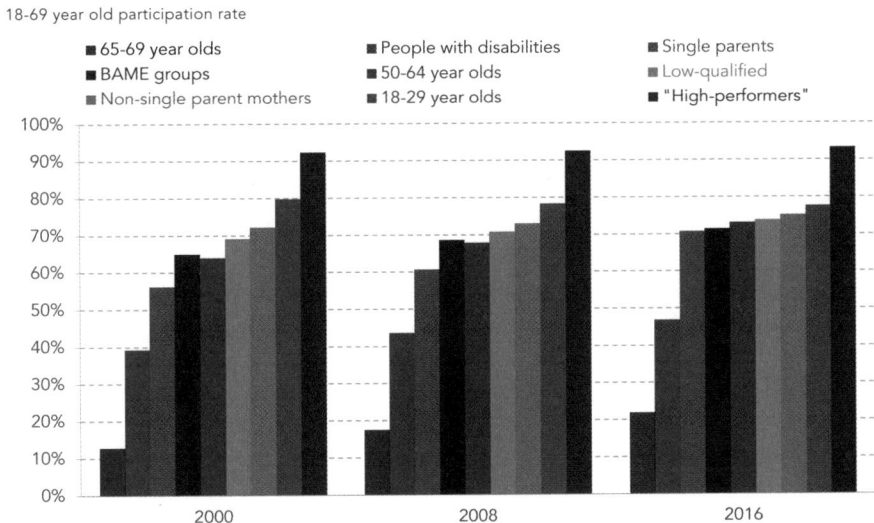

18-69 year old participation rate

- 65-69 year olds
- BAME groups
- Non-single parent mothers
- People with disabilities
- 50-64 year olds
- 18-29 year olds
- Single parents
- Low-qualified
- "High-performers"

Notes: 2000 bars for mothers, low qualified, and single parents represent trends based on slightly different group definitions, indexed backwards from the more recent trends. See Annex 1 of P Gregg & L Gardiner, *The road to full employment: what the journey looks like and how to make progress*, Resolution Foundation, March 2016 for full details.

Source: RF analysis of ONS, *LFS*

for other groups, in particular non-single parents, there has been less change over time.

Scratching beneath the surface of these numbers, Figure 3 suggests that there is nothing inevitable about the relatively poor performance of some groups. Each diamond represents the employment rate for a specific group recorded across 20 sub-regions of the UK, with wide dispersions highlighting the very different labour market outcomes that exist across the country. Variation is particularly marked for people with disabilities, single parents, mothers and ethnic minorities.

Boosting employment rests therefore with both closing inter- and intra-regional gaps in engagement within these 'low activity' groups and narrowing the distance between these

Figure 3: **Labour market outcomes for 'low-activity' groups vary significantly across the country**

Employment rates for different groups in 20 UK sub-regions (18-69 year olds, 2016)

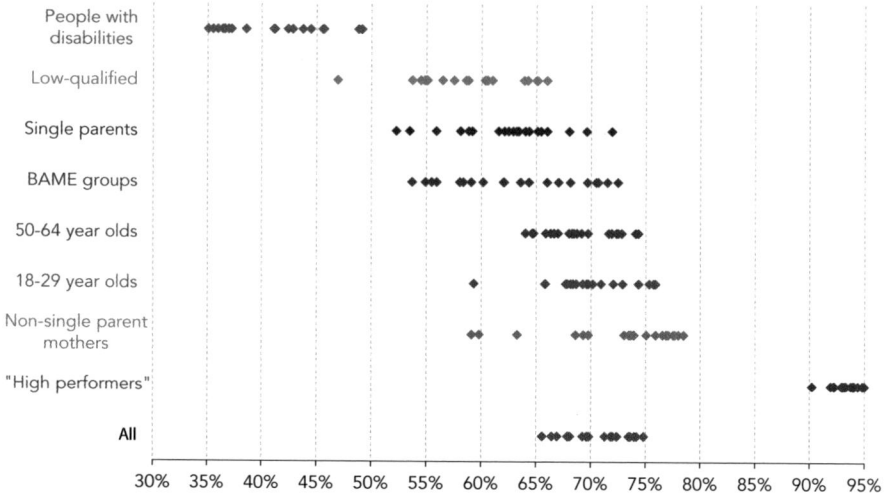

Source: RF analysis of ONS, *LFS*

populations and the 'high performer' group. Previous Resolution Foundation modelling (summarised in Box 1) has concluded that the biggest gains in headline employment numbers are likely to be made by raising participation and employment for the low-qualified, older people and those with disabilities. From a policy perspective, pursuing such goals means identifying both the common improvements that can be made across groups and acknowledging the specific challenges faced by different parts of the population.

In the last chapter we looked at what could be done to increase human capital and in earlier work we have outlined specific proposals to improve labour market outcomes for

---

i Box 1: The employment gains from geographical convergence on 'low activity' performance

In order to assess where the biggest gains in terms of increased labour market participation and employment might be derived from, Gregg and Gardiner[2] undertook a modelling exercise in which they simulated geographical convergence in labour market outcomes across each 'low-activity' group. They focused on outcomes by 2020-21 against an assumed backdrop of trend population growth, trend participation increases and further falls in unemployment.

The convergence they modelled reflected the increase in participation and employment associated with people in each sub-region having labour market outcomes that were equivalent to similar people in the best two performing parts of the country: the East and South East. Clearly employment is boosted by convergence in each of the 'low activity' groups but, as the table below shows, the biggest gains associated with reaching full employment come from improving labour market outcomes for the low-qualified, people with disabilities and older people.

Table 1: Reaching full employment

	Actual (2014-15)	Full employment (2020-21)	Gain
All	30,440	33,030	+2,590
Low-qualified	7,810	9,140	+1,330
18-29 year olds	7,030	7,630	+600
50-64 year olds	8,180	9,100	+920
65-69 year olds	750	990	+240
Single parents	1,430	1,590	+160
Non-single parent mothers	4,350	4,530	+180
People with disabilities	3,380	4,270	+890
BAME groups	3,310	3,800	+490

Notes: For full details of modelling see P Gregg & L Gardiner, *The road to full employment: what the journey looks like and how to make progress*, Resolution Foundation, March 2016

Source: RF analysis of ONS, *LFS*

---

younger workers and mothers.[3] Future research will look at the labour market prospects for BAME groups. Below we focus in more detail on how we can increase labour market participation of two of the groups where much might still be done: people with disabilities and older people. But first we consider two groups where policy has already had a marked impact in recent years – namely single parents and second earners.

Work in Brexit Britain

Policy success and policy threats: the UK's experience on maternal employment

The rise in maternal employment over the last two decades is one of the key success stories of the British labour market, setting it apart from some other advanced economies such as the US. Between 1996 and 2016 the employment rate for (non-single parent) mothers rose by 7 percentage points, while the single-parent rate increased by a remarkable 23 percentage points.

Previous research suggests that these gains were the product of three different policy approaches all pushing in the same direction: improved financial incentives; greater regulation of the employment relationship; and conditionality combined with greater engagement with employment advisors.[4] Going forward, there is much that we can learn from this experience in relation to other 'low activity' groups. But it is important too that we don't row back on these existing successes. In this regard, the fact that one element of this package – financial incentives – is being weakened is a cause for significant concern at a time when changes to our labour market make further increases in labour market participation even more crucial.

The difficulty lies with the roll-out of Universal Credit (UC). This new welfare benefit is gradually replacing the existing tax credits system for lower income working people. The move to a simpler benefit system is to be welcomed, but the current regime of UC being rolled out risks shifting incentives for some groups – particularly single parents and second earners in couples – in a way that puts past gains and future progress at risk.

> The structure of UC also threatens work incentives for second earners in couples – often mothers

Currently, single parents respond strongly to tax credits, with large numbers working precisely the 16 hours a week that constitutes the 'sweet spot' under the system. Here they receive the maximum boost in their tax credit receipt. But the structure of UC – particularly following a succession of budget cuts – means that this 'sweet spot' looks like it will drop to 10 hours (or five depending on housing costs). Once childcare costs are added into the mix, some single parents might conclude that it is no longer worthwhile to work at all.

The structure of UC also threatens work incentives for second earners in couples – often mothers – another group where the evidence is very clear that financial incentives matter. The work allowance available to UC recipients – that is, the amount they can earn before their UC award starts to be removed – applies at the household rather than individual level. It is therefore typically entirely used up by the first earner in a couple, meaning that the family sees reductions in UC support as soon as the second earner starts to earn anything. As a result, around three in ten part-time second earners will lose 70p to 80p of every pound earned.

In order to avoid turning the clock back and instead build on the employment successes associated with tax credits, it's imperative that UC is reformed. We've written in detail on the subject before,[5] about the need for higher work allowances alongside a number of other technical but important adjustments. The success of UC and of ongoing efforts to raise labour market participation depends on getting these details right.

Job retention as well as job entry: rising to the specific challenges of disability and long-term health problems

If the main goal in relation to mothers and single parents is to avoid undermining past gains, the aim for other 'low activity' groups is to replicate these successes. That ambition is certainly reflected in the government's commitment to getting 1 million more people with disabilities into work over the next ten years. This would be a similar number to the overall increase in employment we have seen over the past two-and-a-half years and would take us nearly half way to reaching full employment, based on our estimates in Table 1. But as things stand, government policy in this area is too narrowly focused on the necessary but not sufficient (or indeed always well implemented) task of getting people who are judged to be able to work off benefits and into a job. Figure 4 presents an alternative perspective, showing that more people leave work for health reasons than move into work from health-related inactivity. Moreover, exits from employment have been rising since 2011 and disabled people are more disadvantaged the longer they remain out of work. Non-disabled people are three times less likely to re-enter work if they have been out of a job for a year, whereas someone with a disability is 6.5 times less likely to re-enter work. With this in mind, the government should increase the emphasis it places on job *retention* for those suffering from health problems, alongside a continued focus on job *entry*.

> The government should increase the emphasis it places on job *retention* for those suffering from health problems

For example, building on the success of statutory maternity leave and the crucial lesson that retaining attachment to the labour force through an existing employer is key, workers with health problems should have a new right to return to work following a period of ill-health of up to 12 months, mirroring the right to return for mothers after childbirth. To encourage employers to actively support people back into work, the government should also offer a rebate on Statutory Sick Pay (SSP) where that happens. Keeping workers in touch with the labour market could go a long way to boosting participation among those with disabilities and long-term illnesses.

Of course, while a focus on retention is important, people should not be tied to jobs at all cost. For those leaving employment, support, in the form of the Work and Health programme or other initiatives, needs to kick-in sooner and be more

Figure 4: **Exits from work because of health problems have been rising**

Number giving health reasons as main reason for leaving employment in last six months (18 & over) & number in work giving health reasons as main reason for not being in work a year ago

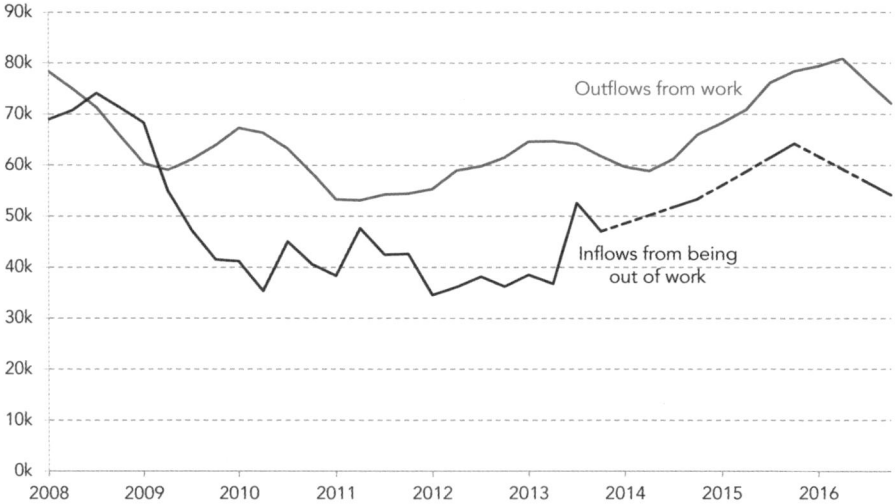

Notes: Dashed lines show linear extrapolation where quarterly data is not available.

Source: RF analysis of ONS, *LFS*

tailored. We provide a fuller outline of these and other proposals in the summary of recommendations.

Financial and non-financial incentives: keeping older people in the labour market for longer

Finally in this chapter, we consider the particular challenges and opportunities associated with raising employment among older people. It should be acknowledged that this is a group for which labour market participation has been rising steadily over time, powered by improvements in health but also the end of the default retirement age and the raising of the state pension age.[6] Despite this, further progress is both desirable and achievable. The labour force participation rate for workers 65 and over is lower than the G7 average. The UK performs better for workers aged 55 to 64 although performance is still below that of many Nordic countries, New Zealand, Switzerland, Japan and Germany. Given that around half the workforce exits employment before reaching state pension age, there is plenty of scope for catch up.[7]

There are of course crossovers with the approach that might be considered for those with disabilities: around a fifth of those aged between 51 and 65 who leave work do so because of health problems. But other factors are at play too.

For example, around 15 per cent of older people are unable to work because of caring responsibilities (compared to around 30 per cent who do not work because of health problems). And, while health problems have been falling over time in this age group, the impact of caring responsibilities has remained constant. The Conservatives have promised to help those with caring responsibilities move into, or return to work. In terms of the former the government could consider allowing those with caring responsibilities to make a statutory request for flexible working immediately, without having to have been employed for 26 weeks. In terms of the latter we would welcome a similar right to return to that which currently exists for those on maternity leave. The Labour party are considering allowing all employees the right to request flexible working, having promised to give all workers equal rights from the beginning of their employment.

In other cases, older people may be discouraged from continuing in work once they reach state pension age. To encourage people to continue working it should be easier for those who have reached state pension age to partially draw down pension pots while continuing to work. Auto-enrolment provides an opportunity for the government to encourage firms to select, and pension providers to provide, schemes that allow for partial drawdown. Leading by example the government should make it easy to partially draw down the state pension and the government should reinstate the option to defer the state pension and take a lump sum (which at present cannot be taken) plus uplift at a later point, both of which were proposed by the Cridland Review.[8] Such a move would be progressive as at present the current deferral arrangements are not very attractive for people with low earnings. Non-financial factors are also important: of those choosing to become self-employed after reaching state pension age the most common reason cited for doing so is job satisfaction.[9]

> Older people may be discouraged from continuing in work once they reach state pension age

Addressing this, more can be done to ensure that older staff have the same opportunities for training and professional development as those younger than them. There should be wider use of mid-life and later-career reviews which the evidence suggests benefits workers as retirement age approaches.[10] Firms are increasingly aware of the need to rethink their approach to staffing and retention to attract and keep older workers. Some large firms – including Barclays, Boots, Aviva and the Co-op – have set themselves targets to employ greater numbers of older workers and are promoting flexible working.[11] Government has a role to play in ensuring that good practice is spread.[12]

Pushing towards full employment requires active government involvement

The UK has made big strides on employment in recent years, but with the labour market at something of a tipping point it is now more vital than ever that we increase participation to reduce the pressures of labour supply constraints. A tight labour market, coupled with an ageing population and lower migration means that firms will need to look beyond their usual pools of talent.

But big gains in employment will not arrive automatically: the government needs to take deliberate action to help people move into, and perhaps more importantly stay in, work. Experience teaches us that policy action in these areas can deliver significant changes in labour market participation – benefitting both the individuals involved and the wider economy.

Getting people into work is only the first step. Wage rises at the bottom of the labour market will help, but for many work is still too insecure and low-quality. What was once seen as a *steadily increasing* feature of the UK labour market – atypical, insecure work – may now be plateauing, but the evidence is that a large chunk of insecurity is here to stay. The next chapter deals with how we tackle this.

Summary of recommendations

— Improving incentives

Recommendation 1 **Increasing work allowances for single parents (to £2,000) and introducing a work allowance for second earners (of £1,500).**

Recommendation 2 **Work allowances for disabled recipients should be restored to the value originally intended, and increased in the future.**

Recommendation 3 **Allow for partial drawdown of the state pension and support expansion of partial drawdown options in private pensions.**

— Keeping people in work

Recommendation 4 **The government should establish a disability employment outflow reduction target.**

Recommendation 5 **The government should explore how it can support those with caring responsibilities, including with promised help for carers moving back into work following a period of caring leave.**

Recommendation 6 **The government should create a unified occupation health architecture including the Fit for Work Service and Access to Work.**

Recommendation 7 **The government should introduce a statutory 'right to return' period of one year from the start of sickness absence.**

Recommendation 8 **The government should offer a rebate on Statutory Sick Pay costs to firms whose employees make a successful return to work from long-term sickness absence within one year.**

— Helping people return to work

Recommendation 9 **Employment support programmes should be available for all those with disabilities, regardless of benefit receipt.**

Recommendation 10 **The Fit for Work Service should have the power to offer early referral to the Work and Health Programme for people unlikely to return to current employment.**

1   P Gregg & L Gardiner, *The road to full employment: what the journey looks like and how to make progress*, Resolution Foundation, March 2016

2   Ibid

3   Ibid

4   P Gregg & D Finch, *Employing new tactics: the changing distribution of work across British households*, Resolution Foundation, January 2016

5   D Finch, *Making the most of UC: Final report of the Resolution Foundation review of Universal Credit*, Resolution Foundation, June 2015

6   J Cribb, C Emmerson & G Tetlow, *Signals matter? Large retirement responses to limited financial incentives*, Labour Economics, Volume 42, October 2016, Pages 203–212

7   DWP, *Fuller Working Lives – Background Evidence*, June 2014

8   J Cridland, *Independent Review of the State Pension Age Smoothing the Transition Final Report*, March 2017

9   RF analysis of ONS, *LFS*

10   The National Voice for Lifelong Learning, *Mid Life Career Review Pilot Project Outcomes: Phases 1, 2, and 3 (2013 – 2015) Final report to the Department for Business, Innovation and Skills*, July 2015

11   O Ralph, *Businesses set targets for recruiting older workers*, Financial Times, 23 May 2017

12   CPID, *Creating longer, more fulfilling working lives: Employer practice in five European countries*, May 2016

Work in Brexit Britain

CHAPTER FIVE

'Atypical' day at the office

Tackling the problems of 'atypical' work

Stephen Clarke

The state we're in

Significant growth in 'atypical' work means one in seven workers are now self-employed, while there are around 800,000 agency workers and 900,000 people on zero hours contracts

While the level of insecure work remains too high it looks to have peaked, with full-time employment accounting for 97 per cent of the jobs growth over the past year

Tax incentives, worth £2,400 for someone costing a firm £30,000, have driven much of the rise in self-employment

What should we do?

Those on ZHCs working regular hours should have a right to a fixed-term contract after three months

The tax treatment of employees and the self-employed should be equalised, as should the benefits

Low-pay protection should be given to some self-employed workers that are price takers, with a new test of whether a 'reasonable' worker would earn the minimum wage

A s well as a big rise in employment the UK has also experienced a large rise in 'atypical' work in the past few years. The number of UK workers who are self-employed, on zero hour contracts (ZHCs) or working through agencies have all increased significantly. This shift has brought with it the benefits of flexibility but serious downsides in lower earnings and a growing part of the workforce operating outside the full protection of employment law.

Much of the debate about this rise in 'atypical' work assumes the growth will continue, viewing it as driven by technological and cultural change. While technology has clearly played a part in growth of some areas of 'atypical' work, not least the gig economy, the evidence is that other factors are significant drivers.

The financial crisis, and the increase in unemployment that followed, provided the backdrop to recent increases in 'atypical' work, indicating a cyclical rather than a purely structural trend. With the recent tightening of the labour market we now appear to be at a tipping point, with evidence that 'atypical' work has plateaued or even fallen in the past year. If low paid labour is less available and relatively more expensive then this is likely to affect the very sectors where 'atypical' work is most prevalent, further reinforcing this tipping point.

However, just as it is wrong to simply assume 'atypical' work will continue to grow in a post-Brexit labour market, so is it to assume that the current high levels will simply unwind or that the status quo is desirable. The evidence is that in places this has become a structural feature of the UK labour market and that flaws in our tax and employment regimes have also driven increases quite apart from the economic cycle or valuable flexibility.

That is why government has a crucial role to play in addressing new developments in the world of work, ensuring workers receive the protection we collectively deem necessary while valuing genuine flexibility. The 'Taylor Review' – established by Theresa May - focuses on this issue. The task is even more urgent in a labour market that needs to become much more productive in its use of lower paid labour as it becomes scarcer and relatively more expensive.

> The Government has a crucial role to play in addressing new developments in the world of work

In this chapter we chart the rise in 'atypical' forms of employment, often (and sometimes wrongly) associated with the rise of the 'gig' economy, set out why this issue still matters as growth in these forms of work starts to plateau, and examine how policy-makers should respond.[1]

'Atypical' work has grown and looks to be here to stay

'Atypical' work is a term open to interpretation, but we use it here to cover those working on ZHCs, those working for an agency or those who are self-employed (with some overlap between these groups). These are the focus of this chapter, but clearly are not the only forms of 'atypical' work, excluding, for example, 'short-hour contracts' guaranteeing people just a few hours a week.

Most people in the UK work as full-time employees. But numbers have shifted significantly in recent years. Since the middle of 2008, the number of people in this position, excluding those who work for an agency or who say they're on a ZHC, has increased by just 1 per cent. Yet, as Figure 1 shows the growth in other forms of employment has been much more rapid. The number of self-employed people has increased by 24 per cent, those working for an agency has increased by 46 per cent and the most dramatic increase has been in the number of people on ZHCs which has risen by over 400 per cent. Such

Figure 1: 'Atypical' work has grown significantly since the financial crisis

Growth in various forms of employment (Q4 2008 = 100)

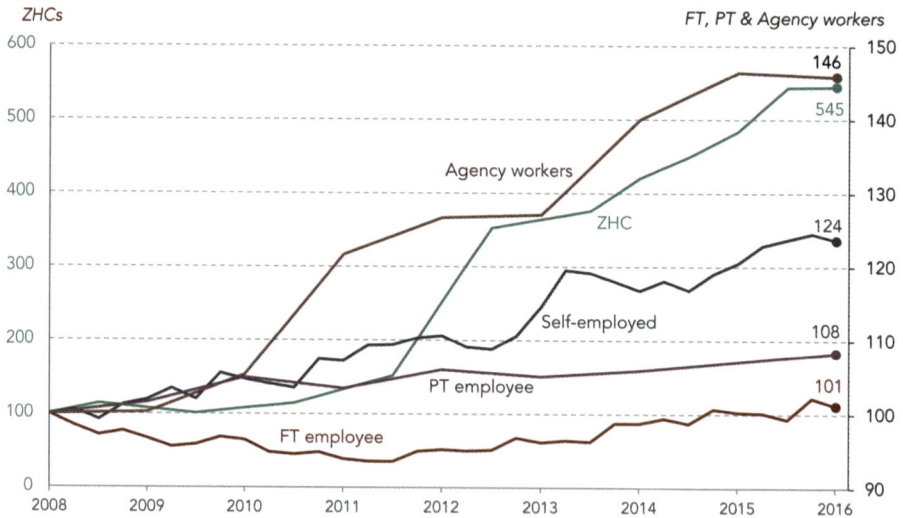

Notes: Full-time and part-time employees, and the self-employed do not include people on ZHCs or working for an agency. The figures for agency workers includes some who are on ZHCs and vice versa.

Source: RF analysis of ONS, *LFS*

increases are stark and represent a significant change to our labour market (although in the case of those on ZHCs some of this is likely to be down to increased awareness,[2] with a dramatic jump in 2013 when widespread media reporting of ZHCs began).

These trends mean that there are now 5 million self-employed workers, 900,000 people on ZHCs and 800,000 agency workers. It is important to note that there is no typical ZHC, agency or self-employed worker. Nevertheless a look at the broad characteristics of workers in these roles (Table 1) suggests that ZHC workers are more likely to be women, younger and less qualified. Agency workers also tend to be less qualified and 40 per cent are migrants. Self-employed workers, which are a bigger and more complex group in some ways, are more likely to be men, older and more qualified. Crucially, earnings tend to be lower on average in all of these 'atypical' forms of work than for full-time employees, even accounting for the different number of hours worked.

Table 1: **Typical 'atypical' workers**

	Female (%)	16 - 29 (%)	50 - 64 (%)	NQF Level 4 and above (%)	Non-UK (%)	Median gross weekly pay
Full-time employee	40	25	25	46	17	£712
ZHCs	54	47	20	30	20	£268
Agency workers	45	32	20	33	40	£500
Self-employed	32	10	35	43	19	£239

Notes: Pay for the self-employed is estimated using data from the Family Resources Survey (FRS)

Source: RF analysis of ONS, *LFS*

This isn't tech-led gigging, but a product of the economic cycle and labour market institutions

There has been much discussion of the growth of the gig economy and the role that technology has played in changing the world of work across the globe. It certainly provides a very visible area in which technology has driven fast growth in forms of work that are far from full time and permanent, but the gig economy and 'atypical' work are far from synonymous (Box 1).

i **Box 1: We've been gigging for a while**

The 'gig' economy brings to mind images of people using technology to rent their homes, order taxis, or sell their artistic wares or programming skills. Some people engaged in these activities are in 'atypical' forms of work (the self-employed jewellery designer on Etsy) others dispute their employment status (Uber drivers and Pimlico plumbers) yet 'atypical' work existed a long-time before anyone used an app. We've long had taxi drivers, plumbers and people selling their crafts in local markets. Technology may have made the issue of the gig economy popular and a subject for discussion but it did not create 'atypical' work.

Crucially the gig economy is far too small to explain the recent growth in 'atypical' work. Wider technology changes, along with increased desire for flexibility from some workers, are more plausible drivers that have clearly played a structural role. But we should be careful about seeing recent UK trends as somehow inevitable.

Firstly that is because inferring from recent economic data that such trends are long-term or inevitable risks missing the role of the economic cycle during the recession and recovery from the financial crisis. As Figure 1 shows, the UK shed full-time work during the 2008 crisis right through to 2011 as GDP fell fast and then bumped along. Meanwhile the exceptional jobs recovery that followed and saw employment reach record highs by late 2014 was made up of big rises in 'atypical' work. While economics text books teach students that increased unemployment and labour market slack during a recession feeds through into wages, it looks likely that in this recession it also exhibited itself through firms feeling more able to demand, and workers being more willing to accept, 'atypical' work.

The reverse of this cyclical effect also comes through in the more recent data; full-time work for an employer has accounted for 97 per cent of the growth in employment in the past year. As also shown in Figure 1, the past year has seen rapid rises in 'atypical' work come to an end. A tightening labour market, with unemployment at its lowest levels since the 1970s and employment at record highs, may not be having the effect the textbooks led us to believe on still stagnant wages. However, they may be giving workers more bargaining power when it comes to the security of work they accept.

The second reason for doubting that global technology trends are driving the rise in 'atypical' work is that we have not seen the same trends in all advanced

Figure 2: **'Atypical' work has grown significantly since the financial crisis**

Change in self-employment as a share of total employment (2001=100)

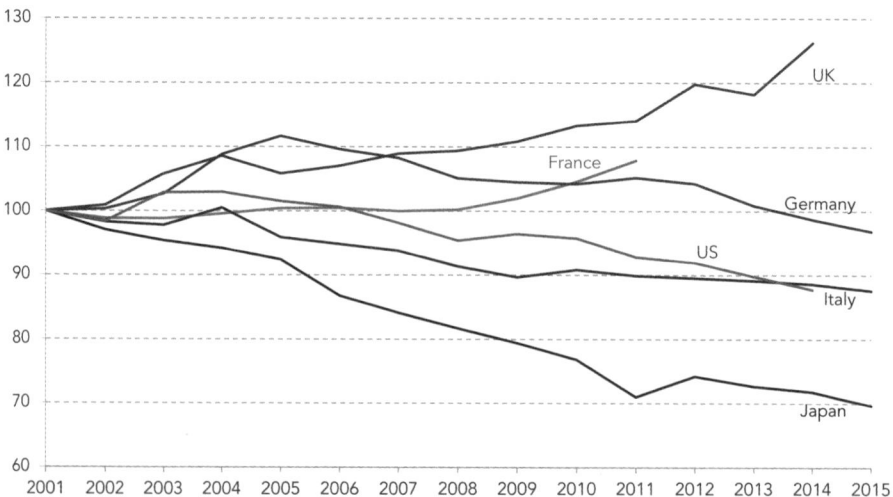

Source: RF analysis of OECD, *Self-employment rate*

economies – especially in relation to the rise in self-employment (see Figure 2). This should encourage us to look at UK-specific labour market institutions, from tax to employment regulations.

A good starting point is the advantageous tax treatment of self-employment in the UK. In terms of the total tax take on a person's labour that costs a firm £30,000, over £2,400 more is received by the exchequer for employees than the self-employed, while the tax benefit of incorporating as an owner-manager is greater still (Figure 3).[3] The majority of this tax difference is driven by the lack of an equivalent of employer National Insurance on self-employed labour which provides a very significant incentive for firms and individuals, especially those with higher incomes, to choose self-employment where they can. Small differences in benefit entitlements

Figure 3: **The tax system favours the self-employed and company owner-managers**

Tax paid on £30,000 of market income, by legal form

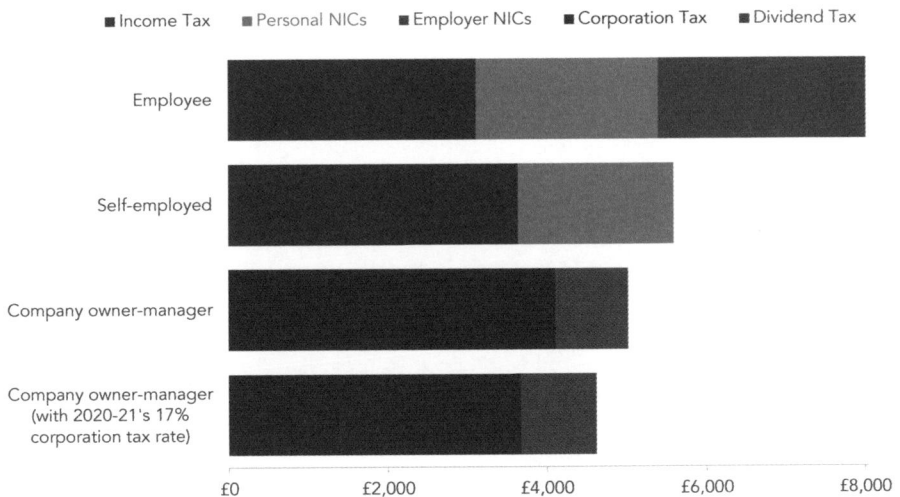

Notes: Based on estimated 2018-19 tax system. Employee salary is £27,400 after employer NICs.

between employees and the self-employed do not come close to justifying such a tax differential, particularly after the introduction of the single tier state pension has removed the single biggest such difference.

Alongside the incentives from the tax system, self-employed workers are not entitled to the minimum wage. As the NLW increases over the next few years this incentive for firms to choose self-employed labour will also rise.

Work in Brexit Britain

There are also financial incentives in employing people on ZHCs: if they do not meet the requisite earnings thresholds staff may not have to be auto enrolled and sick pay is based on hours worked in the past two months which may mean that ZHC workers with fluctuating hours may not be entitled to as much as regular employees. Furthermore agency workers can be paid less than employees (at least for the first 12 weeks).

Addressing high levels of 'atypical' work matters, even if it is no longer rising

If a tightening labour market has started to remove the recent upward pressure on 'atypical' work, should policy makers still care about it? The answer is a clear yes. The sheer scale of such work remains high, it brings with it a pay penalty, it's not clear we have the optimal balance between flexibility for the individual and for firms, and we now have significant uncertainty about classification of self-employed workers in particular. Beyond the labour market there are also major public finance reasons for not believing the status quo is sustainable.

While overall Britain faces a disastrous decade for pay, 'atypical' workers stand out as paying a big financial price when working in this way. These pay differentials are also not simply the product of different job specifications or of the qualification levels of the workers concerned: 'atypical' workers are paid less than regular employees even when the same kind of person is doing the same kind of job. Those on ZHCs are paid approximately 6.6 per cent less than non-ZHC workers, while agency workers face a 'pay penalty' of 2.4 per cent.[4] The earnings of the self-employed have fallen by around 15 per cent in the past two decades, whereas pay for employees is up 14 per cent.[5]

Policy makers will obviously want to recognise that desire for flexibility is a real thing on the part of both firms and workers, with previous surveys having suggested that around eight in ten prefer being self-employed and a (slim) majority of those on ZHCs not wanting to increase their hours.[6] However a significant minority of people would prefer to have a more typical relationship with an employer, and the fact that some large firms, including JD Weatherspoon and McDonald's are finding it necessary to offer more typical work as the labour market tightens points to a desire for more security. In particular there are clearly areas where the flexibility on offer is not genuinely two way and where the case for change is strongest. This is coming out in both legal cases examining the level of control some firms are trying to exercise over workers they argue are self-employed, and in the use of 'zeroing down' the hours offered to ZHC workers or indeed such contracts being used despite someone in practice working the same hours week in week out.

> Desire for flexibility is a real thing on the part of both firms and workers

---

The major tax incentive towards self-employment noted above not only drives much of the increase in the number that are self-employed, resulting in 5 million workers now being largely outside of the protection of employment law, but also has a big cumulative effect on the public finances. By 2020-21 the exchequer will miss out on around £6 billion of National Insurance receipts annually as a result of the favourable treatment of self-employment.[7]

Given this range of considerations it is welcome that we may be witnessing a plateauing of such work as the tightening labour market encourages firms to create more secure forms of employment. However the numbers of 'atypical' workers are still too high. Alongside the impacts above, the type of work on offer also affects how the UK adjusts to the reduction in the supply of lower paid labour that the end of free movement is likely to bring. As the previous chapter sets out, improving the quality of the jobs on offer is part of drawing more workers into the labour force in the first place. It is also one element in helping to create a more engaged and well-trained workforce given that firms are incentivised to invest in their staff because of the lasting nature of their relationship.

> Between three to four in 10 ZHC workers want to work more hours

So what can be done? We focus on addressing the problems associated with ZHCs and self-employment in what follows, with an investigation into how to respond to the challenges facing agency workers a key part of an ongoing research project.[8] In particular we will consider whether or not agency workers are losing their right to equal treatment after 12 weeks without being fully aware that they committing to an annual or Swedish Derogation contract. We will also seek to understand the extent to which agency workers are churned off contracts before 12 weeks, to what extent people are working for multiple agencies, and ultimately how such things are affecting their rights and the benefits they receive.

Ensuring ZHCs provide genuine two way flexibility

Of all the types of 'atypical' work we have analysed ZHCs are associated with the highest levels of dissatisfaction and the biggest pay penalty. Between three to four in ten ZHC workers want to work more hours and interviews with those on ZHCs reveal that many people have difficulties managing their finances, are afraid to demand their employment rights and find it difficult fitting their work around other commitments.[9]

The argument for ZHCs rests on them providing an important part of the UK labour market's flexibility. For students, those with caring responsibilities or complex health needs of their own, or those wanting to work but simply not prepared to commit to given hours, such contracts can allow them the flexibility to vary hours as they wish. But such flexibility must be two way to be justified. There is no strong business case for ZHCs to be used when in practice workers are doing regular hours week in week out and would prefer a regular contract.

We therefore recommend that after three months a worker on a ZHC doing regular hours should have the right to a fixed hours contract guaranteeing them the average weekly hours worked over the previous three months. Three months is an appropriate cut off because it would allow employers to use these contracts for holiday or temporary workers. And crucially, because this is a right, some employees – such as bank nurses – may well choose to continue working on ZHCs because they provide two way flexibility. For reasons of clarity, simplicity, and to allow people who benefit from such contracts to remain on them we favour such an approach over other suggestions of a weaker 'right to request' a contract that reflects the actual hours worked, a different minimum wage rate applying to workers on such contracts, or the outright banning of ZHCs.

> A worker on a zero hours contract doing regular hours should have the right to a fixed hours contract

Of course, as with most labour market reforms there are trade-offs, with risks that while people could still choose to remain or start on a ZHC, a broader reduction in ZHCs may mean that there are fewer flexible options available to those looking for work but who do not wish to accept fixed hours. Government should assess the extent to which this is the case and assist such workers in other ways: the last chapter provided details on how to increase labour market participation by relatively disadvantaged groups.

The reforms above would help address the issue of ZHCs in the private sector, however there are particular issues with ZHCs in the public sector, particularly in care. The majority of domiciliary care workers are on ZHCs, with the move towards ZHCs in the care sector predating the financial crisis and subsequent growth in 'atypical' working.[10] It would be heavy-handed to ban the use of ZHCs in the public sector, but alongside the new right recommended above there is a strong case for local authorities to procure and commission care services with the stipulation that the majority of work is carried out by staff not on ZHCs. It is yet to be seen if the recently announced reforms to care funding will lead to sufficient new investment so that care providers aren't incentivised to rely as extensively on ZHCs.

Reducing the tax incentives towards self-employment

When it comes to reforms relating to self-employment, the clear objective is to provide a level playing field between employment and self-employment, so that individuals and firms can choose arrangements that best reflect their needs and preferences, rather than the tax incentives involved. We should also look again at whether low pay protection akin to the minimum wage can be extended, at least to sub-groups of the self-employed.

Tax action should start with the government returning to the Chancellor's proposal to all but equalise employee and self-employed NICs by raising Class 4 NICs to 11 – or indeed 12 – per cent. This will raise £600 million – or £1 billion in the case of a 12 per cent rate – a year and the change, in combination with the abolition of Class 2 NICs, would mean that the majority of self-employed workers will pay less NI, or none at all.

However, this would still leave a significant tax incentive towards self-employment due to the lack of employer NICs (a 13.8 per cent tax) on self-employed labour. This is difficult to address straightforwardly, but a first step could be to extend employer NICs, or an equivalent levy, to cases where PAYE-registered companies use self-employed labour (including owner-managers) – with allowance made for any input costs (such as materials). The new requirement in the public sector that tackles bogus self-employment by moving the onus for certifying that someone is genuinely self-employed from the individual to the organisation contracting that labour should also be extended to the private sector, beginning with larger companies.

The government's planned further reduction in the corporation tax from 19 per cent to 17 per cent will further increase the incentive to incorporate. Reversing this would be welcome, or else further increases in dividend taxation will be needed to help offset corporation tax falls. To reduce the capital gains tax incentive for incorporating the government could also scale back Entrepreneur's Relief and the Annual Exempt Amount: tax breaks that together cost £6 billion a year and no doubt explain part of the rise of self-employed incorporation.

Strengthening the rights and benefit entitlements of the self-employed

Crucially reform of taxation for the self-employed should be part of a wider package to further equalise not only tax treatment, but also responsibilities and rights.

With the introduction of the single tier pension the most important discrepancy between employees and the self-employed benefit entitlement was ended. The next step should be to offer the self-employed statutory maternity pay (SMP) and paternity pay. Based on their current level we estimate that providing SMP to the self-employed would cost between £9 million and £82 million per annum and that it would cost between £5 million and £18 million per annum to provide the self-employed with paternity pay.[11]

The next step should be to offer the self-employed statutory maternity pay and paternity pay

There are other benefits and rights enjoyed by employees that are not available to the self-employed such as contributory job seekers allowance (JSA), sick pay, and auto enrolment. Previous estimates have suggested that providing the self-employed with contributory JSA would cost around £50 million per annum,[12] while doing so would not be administratively straightforward. One way to provide contributory JSA to some self-employed workers would be to make it available to those who have paid Class 4

NICs at or above a specific profit level (around £25,000) for two years. This would make the contributions required similar to those for employees.

Providing statutory sick pay (SSP) to the self-employed is even more challenging, as it is paid by employers so the government would need to decide if it wishes to spend public money on SSP for the self-employed. Doing so we estimate could cost as much as £340 million – given that the self-employed are more likely to have health problems than employees – but this figure could be higher if the system was open to more abuse than the system for employees.[13] Such a system would necessitate finding an appropriate way to ensure that those claiming were suffering from genuine health problems. GPs may need to play a more active role when issuing fit notes and those in receipt of SSP should be required to take active steps (where possible) to get back to work. Even if SSP is not extended to the self-employed they should be allowed to access the Fit for Work Service.

> Fewer self-employed people contribute to a private pension than do their employee counterparts

Fewer self-employed people contribute to a private pension than do their employee counterparts.[14] There are financial reasons for this; affordability being the most common reason given by the self-employed for not contributing.[15] Raising the earnings of the self-employed (which have been stagnant for two decades) should therefore be a priority. In addition to this more can be done to incentivise saving. The behavioural barriers to contributing to a pension could also be addressed by using an opt-out system when the self-employed file tax returns. Those submitting their tax form online would be required to actively navigate away from contributing to a pension if they did not wish to make similar levels of pension contribution that are required of employees under auto-en-rolment. There are challenges with this approach, not least the selection of a pension provider. Nevertheless this is an idea that has been floated by a number of organisations and merits further investigation.[16] There is also scope for exploring if firms and platforms that rely on self-employed workers could have to auto enrol their workers by default into pension schemes, alongside more radical options of requiring engagers of self-employed labour to contribute directly into pension schemes themselves via a form of levy.

A wider government package could also tackle other issues that particularly affect the self-employed, including the problem of late or unmade payments, perhaps by drafting or tightening laws to ensure that those using self-employed contractors pay them within a similar timescale to employees. A number of local governments in America are bringing in legislation that makes it illegal to not provide a contractually binding payment date to a self-employed contractor or pay them within 30 days. The government should also examine how the operation of the Minimum Income Floor of UC is impacting on the self-employed in practice. The floor is calculated on monthly earnings which may not be appropriate for the self-employed whose earnings may fluctuate more than employees.

Clarifying employment status should not simply be left to the courts and low pay protection extended where possible

Greater clarity is required where the self-employed primarily work for a firm or firms that exert significant control over them. There have been a number of high profile tribunal claims recently where tribunals have decided that those working for companies – such as Uber and Pimlico Plumbers - are not self-employed but workers. That uncertainty is likely to remain for some time, not only because the firms are appealing these decisions but also because they are in industries largely reliant on self-employed labour where the courts will be asked to test other classification questions for years to come.

The Taylor Review may tackle some of these issues by looking at options for a new statutory test for employment status. This would in practice be far from straightforward, but would be welcome given that we should collectively decide how to update our employment laws for the 21st century rather than leaving the heavy lifting to the courts alone. Some, including the Labour party, have also suggested that the law be changed so that it assumes a worker is an employee unless an employer can prove otherwise – switching the onus from the status quo where an individual would have to prove to an employment tribunal that they are a worker. Such contributions are welcome given the challenge for workers in many sectors in accessing employment tribunals, but do not resolve areas where there is a genuine lack of legal clarity.

Beyond questions of correct classification, it is also important to note that low-earning individuals who are classified as self-employed are beyond the protection of the minimum wage. This is a growing challenging as our labour market adjusts to a higher minimum wage in the years ahead. While simply extending the minimum wage to the self-employed is not feasible, there may be ways to extend some elements of low pay protection to groups of the self-employed. We propose that for subsets of the self-employed (those providing commodified labour to price-setting platforms or firms) a test of whether a person working in a 'reasonable' way would earn the minimum wage – similar to the test in the existing National Minimum Wage regulations for workers – could be applied.[17] Deciding which self-employed workers fall into this category would require an assessment of the price-setting power of the firm. Nevertheless this is an idea that should be considered given its potential to discourage firms from paying very low rates to their self-employed workers, with a similar reform having been approved by the Dutch Parliament earlier this year.[18] Crucially this would be in addition to rather than a substitute for ensuring proper employment status classification in the first place.

> Greater clarity is required where the self-employed primarily work for a firm or firms that exert significant control over them

Now is the time to strike a better balance between flexibility and security

A rising wage floor and a fall in the supply of low paid labour will mean that firms will have to change the way that they attract, retain and get the most out of workers. In the new world of work the productivity of the lower paid part of our workforce will come not only from having a flexible workforce but also from having a motivated one, and making sure that the right workers are matched to the right roles. Furthermore, to ensure that the UK has the necessary supply of labour more people will need to be attracted into the labour force by the prospect of good work.

Firms will face a new set of incentives. However government needs to create a regulatory regime that better reflects the changing labour market, and best serves workers and firms. In the past government has rightly focused on getting more people into work – a crucial focus and there is more that can be done in this regard (see the previous chapter). Public policy now needs to ensure that people can progress in work. The problem of progression will grow increasingly acute as the wage floor rises over the next few years, and it is to this problem that we now turn.

Summary of recommendations

— Zero hours contracts

Recommendation 1 **After three months a worker working regular hours on a ZHC should have the right to a fixed hours contract guaranteeing them the average weekly hours worked over the previous three months.**

Recommendation 2 **Local authorities should procure and commission care services with the requirement that the majority of work is carried out by staff on guaranteed hours contracts.**

— Self-employed

Recommendation 3 **The government should equalise self-employed and employee NICs by raising Class 4 NICs.**

Recommendation 4 **As a first step in narrowing wider NI treatment, employer NICs or an equivalent tax should be levied on PAYE-registered companies that use self-employed labour (including owner-managers).**

Recommendation 5 **The new public sector requirement that moves the onus for certifying that someone is genuinely self-employed from the individual to the contracting organisation should be extended to the private sector, beginning with larger companies.**

Recommendation 6 **The government should scrap plans to further lower corporation tax, or else raise dividend taxes to offset this, and should scale back Entrepreneur's Relief.**

Recommendation 7 **Statutory Maternity Pay (SMP) should be provided to the self-employed, costing between £9 and £82 million a year.**

Recommendation 8 **The government should explore if contributory JSA, or something similar, could be available to the self-employed, perhaps for those who have made the necessary contributions.**

Recommendation 9 **The government should assess if Statutory Sick Pay (SSP) can be made available to the self-employed. Safeguards would have to be put in place to prevent abuse.**

Recommendation 10 **The government should explore an opt-out system for the self-employed that encourages the take-up of private pensions.**

Recommendation 11 **A test of whether a 'reasonable' worker would earn the minimum wage could be used to extend low pay protection to certain types of self-employed workers that do not control the price of their work.**

'Atypical' day at the office

1   Many of the growing forms of employment, such as zero hours contracts (ZHCs) and agency work, have been described as 'precarious'. In some respects this is a good description, yet for some people, working for an agency, being on a ZHC, or being self-employed is desirable and financially beneficial (particularly in the case of self-employment) so it would be a misnomer to describe all these forms of work as 'precarious', therefore we will use the term "atypical".

2   Office for National Statistics, *People in employment on a zero-hours contract: Mar 2017*, May 2017

3   D Tomlinson & A Corlett, *A tough gig? The nature of self-employment in 21st Century Britain and policy implications*, Resolution Foundation, February 2017

4   L Gardiner, *A-typical year?*, Resolution Foundation, December 2016

5   A Corlett, *The RF Earnings Outlook Q2 2016*, Resolution Foundation

6   C D'Arcy & L Gardiner, *Just the job – or a working compromise? The changing nature of self-employment in the UK*, Resolution Foundation, May 2014 & D Tomlinson, *Zero-hours contracts: casual contracts are becoming a permanent feature of the UK economy*, Resolution Foundation, March 2016

7   D Tomlinson & A Corlett, *A tough gig? The nature of self-employment in 21st Century Britain and policy implications*, Resolution Foundation, February 2017

8   L Judge & D Tomlinson, *Secret Agents: agency workers in the new world of work*, Resolution Foundation, December 2016

9   M Pennycook, G Cory & V Alakeson, *A Matter of Time: The rise of zero-hours contracts*, Resolution Foundation, June 2013

10   V Alakeson & C D'Arcy, *Zeroing In: Balancing protection and flexibility in the reform of zero-hours contracts*, Resolution Foundation, March 2014

11   We get to this figure by calculating the ratio of female self-employed workers to female employees aged 16 to 50 (0.0967). We also calculate the ratio of self-employed workers to employees reporting that they are on maternity leave (0.0474). These figures are applied to the spend on Statutory Maternity Pay in 2015-16 (£2.3 billion) to derive upper and lower bounds. We then adjust this to take into account the lower earnings of the self-employed using the ratio of median weekly employee pay to self-employed pay (0.64). We then calculate what proportion of people claiming the Maternity Allowance are self-employed (13.7 per cent according to the LFS) and apply this to the spend on Maternity Allowance in 2015-16 (£440 million) to get £60 million. We then subtract this from our initial upper and lower estimates to reach our final upper and lowest estimates. We use OBR data on paternity pay in 2015-16 (£100 million). We then calculate the ratio of male self-employed workers to male employees aged 16 to 50 (0.177) and calculate the ratio of male self-employed workers to employees reporting that they are on paternity leave (0.048). These figures are applied to the estimated spend on Paternity Pay in 2015 (£100 million) to get an upper bound of £18 million and a lower bound of £5 million. We have not estimated what the cost would be if self-employed couples were more likely to make use of statutory shared parental pay than SMP, but if so this would lower the SMP estimate and increase the paternity estimate, lowering the overall cost.

12   S Kennedy & A Seely, *Self-employed people and contribution-based Jobseeker's Allowance*, House of Commons Library, July 2014

13   We calculate this figure by using the ratio of self-employed to employees (0.178) and applying it to the only available estimate of SSP (£1.5 billion in C Black & D Frost, *Health at work – an independent review of sickness absence*, Department for Work and Pensions, November 2011). We then adjust this to take into account that the self-employed are 27 per cent more likely to suffer from health problems that affect the kind or amount of work they can do than employees.

14   Pensions Policy Institute, PPI Response *"Review of automatic enrolment – initial questions"*, February 2017

15   C D'Arcy, *The self-employed and pensions*, Resolution Foundation, May 2015

16   House of Commons Work and Pensions Select Committee, *Self-employment and the gig economy Thirteenth Report of Session 2016–17*, April 2017

17   C D'Arcy, *The minimum required? Minimum wages and the self-employed*, Resolution Foundation, July 2017

18   Lexology, *Statutory minimum wage - for the self-employed as well*, April 2017

CHAPTER SIX

Moving on up

Enabling earnings progression in the UK labour market

David Finch

The state we're in	What should we do?
Many people already struggle to progress out of low pay – three-in-four low paid workers are still there a decade later	Make progression a core part of ongoing government policy, in the same way that raising employment underpins the actions of departments beyond the DWP
The National Living Wage will mean that 4.4 million employees will be earning at, or close, to the legal minimum by 2020, compared to 1.5 million in 2015	Reduce the UC taper rate to increase the incentives for pay progression
Universal Credit (UC) will not solve weak financial incentives to progress at work, many people will keep only 25p of each additional pound they earn	Trial and introduce practical support to help people progress, including job seeking support, skills matching and job brokerage

G overnment labour market policy has focused on two key challenges in recent decades: getting people into work and tackling the worst extremes of low pay. As we've discussed elsewhere in this book, more can and should be done in both these areas. But as the labour market moves into a new era, the country faces a third public policy challenge: boosting the progression of low paid workers onto higher wages, in order to prevent a growing part of the workforce being stuck on the legal minimum.

The National Living Wage (NLW) is building on the success of the National Minimum Wage and helping to reduce the scale of relative low pay in the UK. This is a big shift for the UK labour market, not only because of the change in the relative price of low paid labour discussed in Chapter 1, but also because it will significantly increase the share of the workforce for whom the lower bound represents something of a going rate.

Beyond increasing the number of people on the legal minimum, big rises in the NLW also risk reducing incentives for workers to take on the promotions and job moves that are essential in moving up the pay scale. That is because, with firms facing a variety of labour cost pressures, the risk is that they opt to squeeze wage differentials in the bottom half of the labour market. This matters for the individuals concerned but also has wider implications for firms and national productivity, potentially undermining job matching in the economy.

Building on efforts to bring more people into the labour market by focusing on full employment (Chapter 4) and job quality (Chapter 5), in this chapter we consider what more the government can do to boost pay progression for those already in work.

The UK's policy focus on raising employment and tackling low pay has borne fruit in recent decades

Increasing employment levels and avoiding the long term unemployment and inactivity that emerged in the 1980s has been a core focus of UK labour market and welfare policy for the last two decades. Policy reform has included: stricter work-search requirements and tailored practical support via Jobcentre Plus; improved financial incentives via the tax credit and childcare systems; and labour market regulation to ensure greater equality (such as the right to return to work for mothers). Taken together, these initiatives have proven very successful at both supporting higher employment and ensuring that groups previously at risk of long-term inactivity – particularly single parents – have benefitted.

The UK's remarkable post-crisis jobs recovery has been built on these labour market reforms. As we noted in Chapter 1 however, pay and productivity performance has been much poorer, with average pay not set to return to its previous peak until 2022. Yet the squeeze has been much less pronounced at the bottom end of the labour market, with minimum wage policies helping to protect the pay of the very lowest earners. Indeed, as Figure 1 shows, hourly pay growth towards the bottom (percentile 6; the percentile paid the NLW of £7.20 in 2016 and where pay is higher than 6 per cent of all workers but lower than for 94 per cent) has consistently outpaced growth elsewhere in the distribution (other than the very top which is not shown) since the late-1990s. Each percentile shown represents a position in the distribution of hourly pay for workers across the UK: 'p50' relates to the median or the hourly rate of pay with 50 per cent of workers earning more or less than the amount; 'p90' is the point at which wages are higher than for 90 per cent of employees, but lower than for the top 10 per cent

This period of course coincides with the introduction of the NMW in April 1999, with large real-terms increases in the wage floor during the early-2000s also clearly visible

The UK continues to sit at the wrong end of the low pay league table

Figure 1: **Pay growth across the distribution since 1997**

Indices of real-terms hourly pay in different parts of the earnings distribution: 1997 = 100 (CPIH-adjusted)

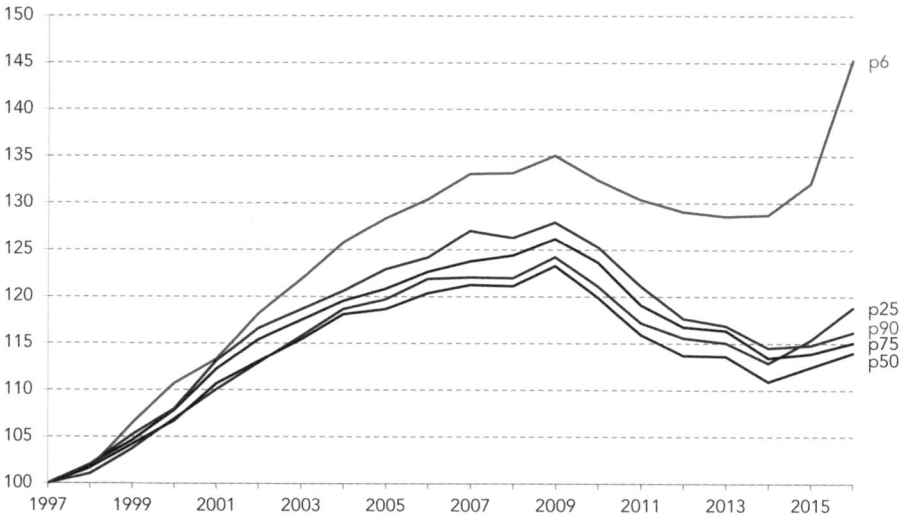

Source: Resolution Foundation analysis of ONS, *ASHE & NESPD*

from the chart. Yet despite the progress provided in terms of eradicating the extremes of low pay, the UK's NMW did little over time to reduce the roughly one-in-five employees considered to be 'low paid' (earning less than two thirds of median pay). Internationally, the UK continues to sit at the wrong end of the low pay league table, with the proportions earning less than two-thirds of median standing at 18 per cent in Germany, 17 per cent in Australia and just 8 per cent in Italy.

Faced with such entrenched low pay, the last government introduced a supplement to the wage floor for those aged 25 and over from April 2016 in the form of the NLW. As discussed in Chapter 1, its influence will grow over the next few years as its value rises relative to typical pay. But even its initial rate on introduction provided a significant pay rise for millions, as is clear in Figure 1. Pay at the sixth percentile of the hourly earnings distribution jumped by 10 per cent in real-terms in 2016, compared with growth of 1.3 per cent at the median and 1.2 per cent at the 90th percentile.

A significantly higher wage floor will compress wages at the bottom

By 2020, the lifting of the value of the NLW to the equivalent of 60 per cent of median pay among the over-24s is expected to produce a pay rise for up to six million workers and the first significant reduction in the UK's level of low pay in the last 30 years.[1] However, its potential effects on productivity and progression are less clear.

Figure 2 shows how, once fully in place, the NLW is likely to affect the pay distribution for workers over-24. Significantly increased bunching at the new floor is clearly apparent, with roughly 8 per cent of employees over-24 expected to be earning £8.75 an hour. In addition, we expect some spillover gains for those paid a little above the floor increasing the total number of affected workers.

Figure 2: **Decreasing returns to progression from low pay compression**

Proportion of workers aged over-24 by pay band

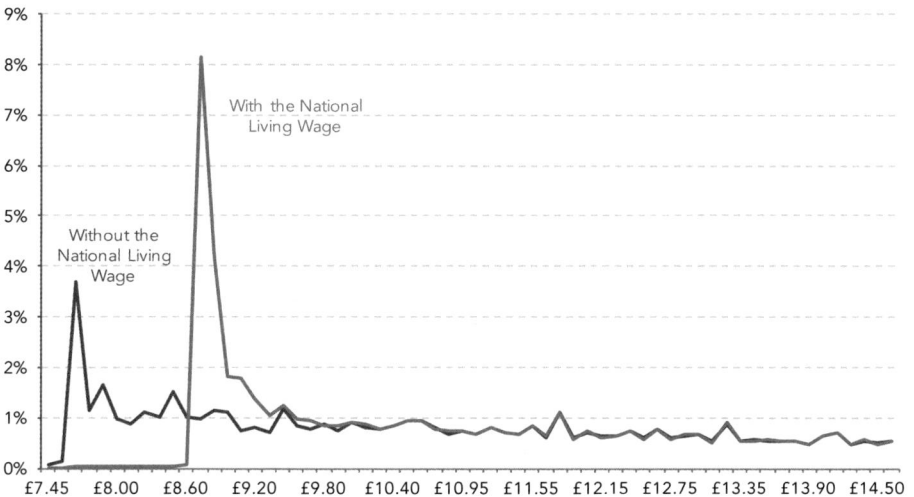

Notes: For detail of assumptions underpinning the impact of the National Living Wage on the pay distribution see A Corlett, et al, Higher Ground, Resolution Foundation, September 2015

Source: Resolution Foundation analysis of ONS, *ASHE & NESPD*

This is a major change for the UK labour market that will mean a big rise in the number of people paid at or near the wage floor. Back in 2000 only around 2 per cent of the workforce (400,000 employees) were on or near the legal minimum (within 1 per cent of it). Even before the introduction of the NLW that figure had already substantially risen to reach 6 per cent (1.5 million) by 2015. It is now set to almost triple to 15 per cent (4.4 million) of all employees by 2020.

In some sectors and regions of our economy the impact of the wage floor and the risk of wage compression will be even more significant. In wholesale and retail the proportion of the workforce paid at the NLW by 2020 is expected to exceed one in four (27 per cent),

Figure 3: **Increasing the share of the workforce paid at or near the wage floor**

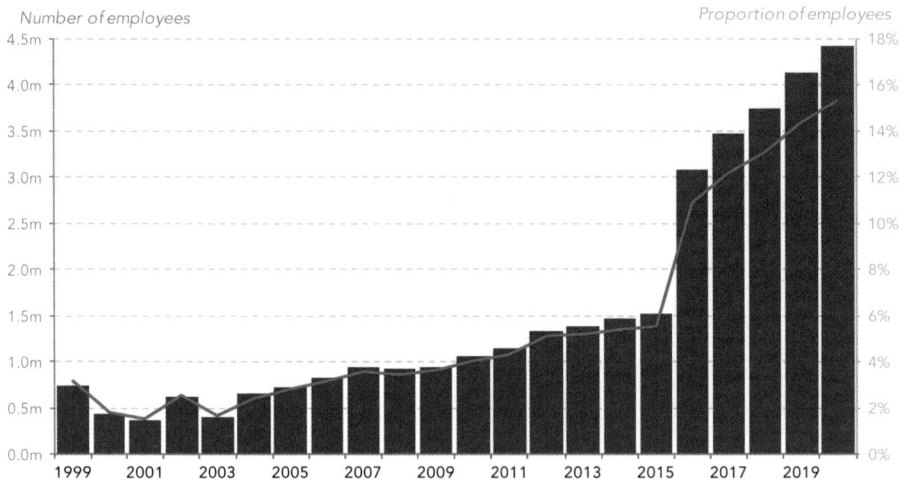

Notes: 'Near the wage floor' is defined as hourly pay being within 1 per cent of the national minimum/living wage

Source: Resolution Foundation analysis using ONS, ASHE, 2015

while the figure for agriculture and fishing is 24 per cent. However, the greatest effect is expected within the accommodation and food services sector where the already high one in four workers (25 per cent) paid at the wage floor is expected to rise to almost one in two (45 per cent). Such variation is also a factor geographically. In some regions, such as the East Midlands and Wales, a fifth of workers are expected to be on the wage floor by 2020, rising from 8 and 7 per cent respectively.

A growing share of our workforce being on the legal minimum raises new progression challenges

Why does it matter if the general level of pay received by lower earners is so much higher than it would otherwise be and we see a very welcome reduction in overall pay inequality in Britain? The answer lies within the dynamic nature of the labour market.

Earning relatively little – whether just below or just above the official 'low pay' line – is clearly less of a problem for those for whom it is a staging post on the way to higher earnings. But a lack of progression from low pay was already a problem in Britain before the introduction of the NLW. For too many workers, low pay is a lasting norm. Previous Resolution Foundation research has shown that three-quarters of low paid employees are still in low pay a decade later.[2] Key factors to escaping this position include moving

Work in Brexit Britain

job, consistently remaining in employment and obtaining a degree. However, as we move into a new era for the labour market, the first appears to be occurring less frequently than it used to and the wage returns associated with the second and third have been falling.[3]

Further compression of the pay scale could make it harder still to move away from the wage floor, with important rungs in the pay ladder effectively stripped out. To the extent that narrower pay differentials reduce the returns associated with taking on additional responsibilities following promotion or a job change, the higher wage floor might also act as an unintended disincentive to progression.[4] Likewise, wage compression could reduce the signalling effect associated with wages. This would mean reduced labour mobility, with workers less likely to move into roles that best match their talents, and negative implications for aggregate productivity.

Of course, the flip side to this is that the lifting of the wage floor could serve as a spur to productivity gains. As we have discussed throughout this book, increases in labour costs towards the bottom end of the labour market should be providing firms with a clear incentive to invest in technology and human capital in order to boost output per hour worked. But the fact that firms are facing a number of labour market challenges simultaneously – including auto-enrolment roll-out, the introduction of the apprenticeship levy and a labour supply shock following the EU referendum – means that one potential response is to meet extra costs at the bottom end of the workforce by squeezing pay and conditions in the middle of the distribution.

> The lifting of the wage floor could serve as a spur to productivity gains

Government can clearly help in this area – both in terms of reviewing the interaction between pay and welfare and in terms of practical career progression support services. At the very least, government should take this growing issue seriously as a major new challenge for our labour market and avoid making things worse – something that current policy direction is in danger of doing.

Creating the right incentives to progress

The current (though soon to be superseded by Universal Credit (UC)) tax credit regime has shortcomings, but played an important role in both raising the incomes of families with children and increasing employment since it was developed in the early-2000s. A strong financial incentive to enter work (in the form of an additional in-work payment for recipients once they meet an 'hours rule' requirement for certain hours of work per week) has helped boost employment. Single parents in particular have responded strongly, with significant numbers working precisely the 16 hours a week required to achieve the extra payment.[5]

The next natural step for welfare reform to take, that of supporting people to move into full-time work and to progress, started to be trialled in the mid-2000s. This came in the form of the Employment Retention and Advancement (ERA) initiative a key part of which comprised time-limited payments conditional on people remaining in full-time work

These moves took a backseat with the onset of the financial crisis, but need restarting now in reaction to the changes that are underway in our labour market. The good news is that we can be fairly confident that a mix of incentives, conditions and support for those in work can have an impact. Indeed recent findings from one part of the ERA trials, in which single parents entering work were paid a time-limited credit if they remained in full-time work for a specific period of time, showed that those in the trial were not only more likely to work but to work full-time, rather than part-time, hours. It was not just the size, but the shape of incentive that proved important to its success.[6]

Future government action to support progression will take place in the context of the new benefits system – Universal Credit. UC remains a vehicle for possible radical reform, with its key objective of combining six different benefits into one, potentially offering big gains in terms of simplicity and in easing the transition into work. We discussed how incentives in UC can be improved for people entering work in Chapter 4 – including ensuring that we do not see big reductions in the average hours new entrants choose to work – but more could also be done to improve incentives to progress once employment is secured.

As with current in-work support, UC entitlement is reduced as a family's earnings increase. Originally this was intended to be at a rate of 55 per cent, but this 'taper' currently sits at 63 per cent. That means that a worker keeps only 37p of each additional pound earned, falling to 25p when also paying income tax and National Insurance. For some (those currently entitled to housing benefit and tax credits) this means incentives to progress onto higher rates of pay have been increased, given some very high taper rates in the existing benefits system. However, incentives to progress for many of those receiving UC can remain every bit as weak as those under tax credits and, in the case of second earners, can be weaker.

> Universal Credit remains a vehicle for possible radical reform

By way of example, Figure 4 sets out the gains to net income from hourly pay rises for a full time worker on the wage floor (assumed to be £8.75 in 2020) who is in a couple with two children. The figure depicts two scenarios, one where only tax and National Insurance are paid on additional earnings, the other where they are also on UC and seeing their benefit entitlement reduced as net earnings rise.

Because we assume the main earner is already in full-time work, there is no remaining work allowance (the amount a family can earn before their UC award starts to be withdrawn). With the UC taper therefore applying to every extra pound earned, alongside tax and National Insurance deductions, they keep as little as 25p of each additional pound earned. For example, across a year a pay rise of £1 an hour would mean an increase in gross earnings of £1,950 a year but an increase to net income of only £500.

This stands in stark contrast to the example of a person who increases their hourly pay but is not on UC. In this scenario, paying only income tax (20 per cent rate) and National Insurance (12 per cent rate) the worker keeps 68p an hour of each extra £1 an hour earned. If working full-time and across a year that equates to an increase in net income of £1,350 from the same annual gross pay rise of £1,950. The incentive to progress and secure a £1 pay rise above the legal minimum is nearly three times weaker in this example for someone on UC than it is for a worker not receiving UC.

Figure 4: **The return to a pay rise under Universal Credit**

Net income gain per hour worked for given hourly pay rise for a main earner on the wage floor in a couple with two children and rent of £130 a week

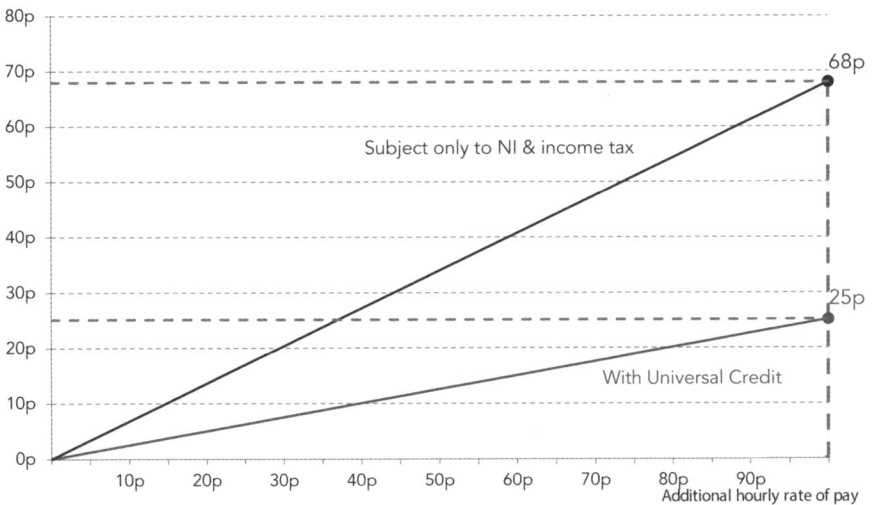

Source: Resolution Foundation analysis using the RF microsimulation model

In order to assess what shape and size of financial incentive is most effective in encouraging progression at work, the government should commit to a long term program of trials to ascertain the impact of such rewards. Such trials should begin as soon as possible given that they are likely to take time. In the shorter term the government should reduce the UC taper from 63 per cent.

Going beyond the job centre

It is important to note that in one key respect the government has already moved to set progression within the labour market, rather than simply entry into it, more firmly on the agenda. UC introduces a concept of in-work conditionality. Put simply this extends the work-search requirements currently imposed on unemployed people claiming benefits to those with low levels of earnings. The primary aim is to set an expectation that benefit recipients achieve a level of earnings equivalent to full-time hours at the minimum wage, or part-time if the individual has caring responsibilities or is deemed to have limited capability for work.

This element of UC means that Job Centre Plus (JCP) will play a new role in encouraging progression for those receiving benefits in work, rather than focusing solely on the unemployed. However this welcome shift is likely to be limited by a number of factors. First, the focus of support remains on hours worked which, while an important route to progression for some, is too narrow and is likely to miss the key question of this chapter – how to deliver pay progression. Secondly, it is unclear if JCP has the resources to fully fund a program of in-work support given ongoing cuts to the DWP budget and a potential push to reach full employment. Finally, there are valid concerns about the extent to which working people are reluctant to continue interactions with JCP once they have found work.

Crucially a push on progression requires going beyond DWP customers. Although UC provides an opportunity to facilitate interaction with many low paid workers, some of whom will previously have had little or no contact with JCP, not all people in need of a pay boost will be entitled to UC and so many will remain outside of the system. For example, many workers on the wage floor with low housing costs and without children will not be in receipt of UC, but are a key group likely to be affected by the growing progression challenge set out above.

Progression support for people in work is not widely available either in the UK or internationally, but it does exist. Some of this is run by the public sector, with the aforementioned UK trials having some successes and providing a base of evidence on which to build.[7]

In other cases private initiatives have had an impact: the Living Wage Foundation provides support for participating employers to maximise the gains for their business of voluntarily paying wages above the legal minimum through increased productivity and improved retention. Similarly, Timewise helps workers, usually mothers, to find better paid forms of part-time or flexible work, often utilising a job brokerage model to encourage employers to adapt advertised roles into flexible ones that are attractive to a ready supply of skilled applicants. Such initiatives recognise both that the role of employers is vital in rising to the progression challenge, and that for many people progression will come as a result of moving jobs.

It might be argued that given these wider considerations, JCPs new focus on in-work conditionality should be extended to providing wider progression support. We do not support such an approach however. We recommend that JCP retains a focus on supporting sustained employment outcomes but we do not believe it should be the main provider of progression support. Planning a career trajectory should form a core part of the conversation between out-of-work recipients and JCP, as should maximising pay when searching for a role, but the focus in this relationship should remain primarily on finding employment.

> Beyond Universal Credit, an ambitious and extensive co-ordinated programme of progression trials should be started

One clear additional role the UC system should play is in actively identifying long-term low paid individuals – especially at key life transition points (such as when a youngest child starts school) – who are not subject to in-work conditionality (for example because they are already working full time on the NLW) to offer and direct them to wider progression support.

Beyond UC, an ambitious and extensive co-ordinated programme of progression trials should be started. Providers would aim to deliver a sustained boost to earnings for individuals, drawing on the past success of programmes such as ERA in the UK and others internationally, and linking practical support to the right mix of financial incentives and conditionality.

Importantly, although being entitled to UC or earning below a given conditionality threshold should not preclude an individual from engaging with pay progression support, such activity should not be mandated by JCP.[8]

It is likely that many of these trials will be run locally, however there are concerns over the capacity of local areas to deliver such new forms of support at scale. Given this, close ties to JCP and Local Enterprise Partnerships (LEPs) are needed alongside forms of national oversight.

Progression on a national level

Alongside these local collaborations, a national body should oversee and commission new forms of support, build a strong evidence base (perhaps in conjunction with a What Works Centre for progression), and promote best practice. In addition such a body could ensure that progression is recognised as a key area of government policy, as boosting employment is now. Such an approach would recognise both the importance of this progression challenge for our economy, but also the fact that while we have some knowledge of what works there is much more to learn.

In the UK a National Careers Service already exists, although provision is often considered to be ineffective. This is emblematic of a deeper historical problem in the UK where – with the exception of graduates in some fields – we have continuously failed to provide an effective link between education and employment. We discussed the role of non-graduate training and career routes in Chapter 3, but it is clear that more also needs to be done, particularly to provide guidance for people outside of any formal education or training.

The national progression body could help address this problem. The body could provide clear and accurate information about opportunities and rewards to progression through specific career paths, and at a far more granular level than the advice currently provided by the National Careers Service. A detailed assessment of the number of jobs, vacancies and pay scales of different roles within sectors would help raise individuals' awareness of opportunities. Such provision is possible; the Career Pathway Maps developed by the Minneapolis innovation network being one such example.[9] Such a service could make it easier for people to look for work outside of their local area, something low-paid workers rarely do.

A further, crucial, role for this body would involve engagement with employers. Current engagement tends to occur at a local level, which makes sense when considering opportunities in local labour markets. But the incidence of low pay is highest in specific sectors, and these cut across regional boundaries. To effect change at a national level it is therefore vital that employers are engaged at a sectoral rather than local level, to ensure that progression is built into future workforce plans.

Meeting the new policy challenge of the new era

Having once been an international laggard on employment, the UK now enjoys an enviable reputation for getting people into work. This turnaround hasn't occurred by accident, but is a product of sustained proactive intervention which has evolved over time. The UK has also taken a lead on tackling low pay via the development first of the NMW and now the NLW. The country's low pay problem has far from disappeared, but the strength of effective labour market institutions has been demonstrated very clearly once again.

With the labour market undergoing profound change – driven by rising costs at the bottom end of the market and a significant labour supply shock associated with Brexit – it is time for public policy to stand up again. In particular, government must react to a new challenge – that of progression. To do so, a change in mind-set is needed, and with this a change in the direction of policy. Reform will take time. After all, it took two decades to get the high employment flexible labour market of today, and it may take another two to shift business models towards higher paying approaches. But there is no reason why the UK cannot once more stand in the vanguard of progress.

Summary of recommendations

— Universal Credit

Recommendation 1 **Improve financial incentives in UC by gradually reducing the taper while testing different levels and shapes of financial incentive.**

Recommendation 2 **The role of in-work conditionality within UC should be limited to full-time working, with reduced hours for those with caring responsibilities or limited capability for work, rather than relying on JCP to take on a wider progression role.**

Recommendation 3 **Out-of-work UC recipients should be encouraged to consider any work search requirements as a step on a longer career path to a higher rate of pay or number of hours worked.**

Recommendation 4 **Use Universal Credit administrative data to identify long term low paid individuals, or those at risk of low pay, and signpost them to progression support, targeting individuals at key life stages.**

— Practical support to progress

Recommendation 5 **Deliver, trial and test practical forms of support to help people progress, drawing on what UK evidence already exists, and examples from elsewhere. Delivery should overlay current channels via Local Authorities, Local Employment Partnerships and JCP.**

Recommendation 6 **Dramatically improve the career guidance information available to individuals including far greater mapping of jobs, vacancies and pay scales by sector and occupation.**

— Focusing on progression at a national level

Recommendation 7 **Create a national body to oversee progression trials, ensuring that they are of high quality and keeping track of what works to ensure best practice methods are spread.**

Recommendation 8 **Work with employers at a sectoral, rather than simply local, level to ensure that progression is built into future workforce plans.**

Recommendation 9 **Ensure that progression is a core part of ongoing government policy, in the same way that employment underpins the actions of departments beyond the DWP.**

1   C D'Arcy & A Corlett, *Taking up the floor: Exploring the impact of the National Living Wage on employers*, Resolution Foundation, September 2015

2   C D'Arcy & A Hurrell, *Escape Plan: Understanding who progresses from low pay and who gets stuck*, Resolution Foundation, November 2014

3   L Gardiner & P Gregg, *Study, Work, Progress, Repeat? How and why pay and progression outcomes have differed across cohorts*, Resolution Foundation, February 2017

4   C D'Arcy & A Hurrell, *Escape Plan: Understanding who progresses from low pay and who gets stuck*, Resolution Foundation, November 2014

5   The 'sweet spot' we discussed in Chapter 4.

6   M Brewer & J Cribb, *Lone parents, time-limited in-work credits and the dynamics of work and welfare?*, Institute for Social and Economic Reseach, January 2017

7   Ibid

8   Although time used to engage with such support should be taken into account when setting work search requirements.

9   Minneapolis Saint Paul Regional Workforce Innovation Network, *Career Pathway Maps*, 2017

Conclusion

Predicting change can be a dangerous business, but preparing for it is prudent. There are signs that the UK labour market is at a tipping point, one that is likely to have a significant impact upon workers, firms and the economy. Fortunately the start of a new parliament means that the new government has the opportunity to chart a course to shape the labour market for the future.

We have detailed the shifts that are underway. Despite sluggish pay growth overall, a look towards the bottom of the labour market shows that – powered by the National Living Wage – wages and labour costs are rising. Furthermore this comes at a time when we are on the cusp of a shock to the supply of low-wage labour. Foreign-born workers have accounted for two-thirds of all employment growth since 2012. They form a sizeable minority – in some cases even a majority – of employees in some sectors. While Brexit itself is some years away, continued uncertainty over the status of foreign-nationals, a weaker pound and tighter labour markets in continental Europe, mean that it may not be long until the supply of migrant labour falls noticeably. Indeed net migration is already showing signs of decline, and this is before free movement comes close to ending.

Firms most reliant on such labour will need to adjust to this brave new world, which comes at a time of broader upheaval; in the country's trading relationships, laws and regulations, as well as other cost pressures such as the continued expansion of auto enrolment. Some will take the opportunity to change their business models and will successfully adapt, potentially raising productivity in the process. Others may struggle.

Firms will lead the process of change, but government can increase the chances of success and is responsible for setting the framework for our labour market within which workers and employers operate. The new government should start by providing more clarity for firms and employees, in particular by setting out a vision for a new immigration system by the end of the year. Such clarity can help business, on whom the onus falls to make long-term plans for investments in staff and machines.

There are also many areas where government and industry's combined efforts will be needed. The UK's recent impressive employment performance has left unemployment at forty year lows, meaning that firms seeking to adjust to the labour market changes of the coming years will need to look towards hiring workers from a broader pool of applicants. Government has a role to play in making that possible by encouraging greater participation among those furthest from the labour market. Similarly government must ensure that the welfare state is equipped to support people in this new world of work, and that if firms create the opportunities, people have the incentives and skills to take advantage of them.

Our employment law needs to be updated to better reflect the 21st Century world of work. We need to make more productive use from a reduced pool of relatively more expensive low paid labour. For these reasons the Government should use the Taylor Review to act on excessive levels of insecurity in the workplace and ensure that the very real benefits of flexibility are enjoyed by both employers and workers.

Change can be risky, but it also creates opportunities. After nearly a decade in which discussions about the UK labour market have focused on the effects and aftermath of the financial crisis, new challenges are emerging. Brexit is obviously top of that list, but it is not the end of it. Stepping back, recognising those new challenges and answering them is how we ensure our labour market is able to continue delivering the rising living standards on which Britain's families depend.

Acknowledgements

This work contains statistical data from ONS which is Crown Copyright. The use of the ONS statistical data in this work does not imply the endorsement of the ONS in relation to the interpretation or analysis of the statistical data. This work uses research datasets which may not exactly reproduce National Statistics aggregates.

As part of the research for this publication ComRes interviewed 503 business decision makers employing EU/EEA workers online between 12th and 26th April 2017. Data were weighted to be demographically representative of GB businesses by number of employees.

For their support in this research we would like to thank Unbound Philanthropy.

For their contributions to chapter two the authors would like to thank Jonathan Portes, Professor of Economics and Public Policy at King's College, and Harvey Redgrave, Director of Strategy and Delivery at Crest Advisory. The authors would also like to thank Lee Osborne at the NFU and the firms in the agricultural sectors that agreed to be interviewed as part of the research. The author would also like to thank Dan Holden, Consultant at ComRes.

The authors would like to thank the Department for Education for providing the Employer Skills Survey (ESS) data used in chapter three.

For their contributions to chapter six the authors would like to thank Jane Mansour, independent policy consultant, Tony Wilson, Director of Policy and Research at the Learning and Work Institute, and all those who attended the progression and Universal Credit roundtable at the Resolution Foundation in January 2017.